Learning to Use
Your Bible

THE DISCIPLESHIP SERIES

Learning to Use Your Bible

LEADERS MANUAL

OSCAR E. FEUCHT

Concordia Publishing House
Saint Louis   London

The Discipleship Series

A BASIC CHRISTIAN LIBRARY
To Equip Today's Christians
for Their Role as CHURCH

Learning to Use Your Bible
Christians Worship
The Christian's Mission
Christian Family Living
The Church Since Pentecost

These practical, learn-by-doing paperbacks focusing on the skills of Christian living were written at the direction of the Board of Parish Education of The Lutheran Church — Missouri Synod

Bible quotations in this study are from the Revised Standard Version unless otherwise noted

Concordia Publishing House, St. Louis, Missouri
Concordia Publishing House Ltd., London, E. C. 1
© 1969 Concordia Publishing House
Library of Congress Catalog Card No. 77-76228

MANUFACTURED IN THE UNITED STATES OF AMERICA

Contents

Introduction

The books of the Discipleship Series form a basic library on practical Christianity. A living relationship to Jesus Christ expresses itself in a number of ways: in the Christian use of the Bible, in a life of worship, in Christian family relations, in accepting life as a mission, and in active membership in the church, the body of Christ.

This series came into being to fill a widely felt need.

In outline form these courses were taught in a number of churches. The favorable response led to the development of full-length books designed to form a Christian's small personal library. We envision their use by individuals for private reading and by groups for class study and discussion. In the latter case, the greatest benefits will be received when the material is discussed under a competent leader who supplies the stimulation and supplementation which only a teacher-leader can give.

The student's role is to read each chapter twice, once before class to get the full sweep of its message, and a second time after class to look up such additional references as the student may desire or need. Because these are skill courses, related daily readings are supplied. Skills cannot be learned without practice. Make this a learn-by-doing course.

High school and college students spend whole semesters mastering a difficult text and doing laboratory work. No less effort is needed for the continuing growth of the adult Christian. The leader's role is to motivate and involve his class so that each person is persuaded to do serious work.

The leaders manual supplies teaching outlines, additional background, new ideas for procedure, and alternate approaches. Choose procedures you will feel comfortable with. Use fresh approaches suited to achieving the session goal. The leader's greatest temptation will be to do the learning for his class. Help the student discover for himself. Some key passages are printed out in the study text to save the reader's time. Other passages should be looked up as need determines. Some facts are repeated at various points. This provides for built-in review and restatement. The goal is to give the student a total view of Scripture.

The leader will need to glance at the following chapter in order to make advance individual and class assignments. Equally important is getting one or two reports in each session from the students to develop their study morale. Allow freedom for student questions, comments, and observations. As the class feels free to talk, it becomes a learning fellowship, a student-teacher-God trialogue.

The field testing of this course indicated that it is best to begin with personal reading and study skills before taking up such broader subjects as nature and form, interpretation principles, and an overview of the two Testaments. The field test also showed that Chapters 7 to 12 demand two class sessions to deal adequately with content and to pace the learning for persons in the class. You may thus offer a 6-session first course (Part One) and a 12-session second course (Part Two).

The sketches of the Old and New Testament books and the chart of the Old Testament were added to augment the study text and make the book a permanent reference work for the student. The average Christian needs help in finding the distinctive message of each book. This is especially the case with the Old Testament books. It is hoped that these supplements will be used frequently as keys to the Bible library.

The reference books given at the end of each chapter are chosen with lay leaders and students in mind. Those with a double asterisk (**) in the leaders manual appear also in the study text. Those with a single asterisk (*) indicate the author's choice where a larger reference library is not available. *A selected group of basic books should be assembled for this course and made available for class use.* At the close of the course the books may be put into the church library.

As a leader of this course you have one of the most challenging assignments you have ever received. You can open the Bible for your students as it has never been opened to them before. You can enrich them for the rest of their lives. He who gives skills does more than he who imparts knowledge. He who gives vision contributes more than he who drills facts. Here is your call to distinctive service for your Lord. You will become richer than your students.

Chapter 1

Personal Use of the Bible

Aim and Scope

The purpose of this session is to help your students develop the practice of living daily with their Lord. Does this sound as if we are "trying to escape from life," as some critics would put it? At times we seem to make religion "a mechanism to escape into another world." Let us acknowledge the need of getting the spark and vitality only Christ can give. He gives us daily renewal through personal use of His Word. Luther speaks of daily renewal of faith under the fourth part of Holy Baptism in his Small Catechism.

The moods of our times are not conducive to this kind of living. Yet millions of believers in their darkest hours and under the greatest tensions have found in Christ's words the peace, hope, and courage needed to carry their greatest burdens and win their greatest victories. Many modern books (*The Organization Man, Lord of the Flies*) and many dramas and movies are built around the dilemma of modern man who finds himself at wits' end. We Christians know that healing is to be found for all people in all conditions of life in the Gospel's gracious words of life. (John 6:63)

The aim of this session is to help your class realize what it means to "practice God's presence" (not merely to assert it), part I; to live each day by the Word of God (Matt. 4:4), finding God's message for each situation in the rich spiritual storehouse of the Scriptures, part II; and to recognize that "man is what he thinks," part III. If he thinks God's thoughts, it will make all the difference in the life he lives.

Our modern generation needs the vision, insights, purposes, directives, and spiritual power which only God's words can give. They sustain us spiritually, mentally, and, as many a physician will testify, in some instances also physically.

How Will You Teach the Lesson?

Some experiences will need to be related by class members and leader. Ask for personal testimonies or evidences of God's nearness. Personalize this lesson. As much of the lesson as possible should be built around a deeper look into Bible passages referred to. You might ask: "Have you ever found yourself in Peter's place, faint with fear, even when the Lord has invited you to come to Him?"

With the chapter in the study text, the outline of the lesson in the leaders manual, and your own experience in the Christian life, you are equipped to teach and to enlist the class in discovering meaning (in the selected Bible passages) and in sharing what the Word of God has done for you and them.

A teaching outline is supplied for each chapter. It generally follows the chapter structure. Designed for the teacher-leader, it is very useful to place on the chalkboard before the session begins. It helps pace the class session, supplies constant focus, and shows what progress is being made. It helps keep the whole chapter before the class.

One of the best ways of preparing for a class session is to carefully read the chapter, make marginal notes as new ideas or illustrations come to mind, and then prepare a teaching outline. In doing so, choose approaches or methods that will fit class and subject matter and that will develop conversational, dialogical teaching-learning. This can make every class session a new adventure.

Leave space on the chalkboard for fill-ins from the class. At the end of the class period the class sees the contributions of both teacher and class. The leader should always feel free to be himself, to adapt and make the chapter his own. This is the secret of live teaching.

Teaching Outline

The "three books"; three examples: schoolteacher, Mueller, Moody

I. *Taking God into Our Lives*

Knowing God (not merely a book), Eph. 3:16-19
Practicing His presence

Lives barren without Him, Ps. 10:3-4
Regaining Christian poise, Eph. 1:18-20; 2 Cor. 5:17
Personal devotions: being with Him in modern complex living, Eph. 3:16
Daily worship of Him – not Sunday only
You are the initiator

II. *How the Bible Helps Us*

Through the power of Psalm 23
Through use of many reading lists and suggestions (exhibit examples)
The lists at the end of the lesson (practice)
A "thought for the day" approach (an example)
"Help in Time of Need" (joy, trial, fear, worry, death)

III. *Christ and His Word Sustain Us*

"Lost" in God's world
"As a man thinks," Prov. 23:7; Luke 11:33-36
Life and security in Christ, John 10:10
Christ the Bread of life

Overview of the Session

1. Welcome the class and group worship
2. Introduce the study book and explain the course
3. Introduction to lesson
4. Lead the class through the lesson (I, II, III)
5. Assignments for daily readings and next session
6. Closing "thought for the week"

Teaching the Lesson

1. Welcome the Class

Introduce each member. Then introduce yourself. Have a secretary pass a ruled tablet around on which each person writes his or her name and address. See that everyone is comfortably seated in a way that is conducive to participation – for instance, in a circle or semicircle. Tablet-arm chairs will be helpful. Keep the introductory period short, but make it warm and cordial. Express your own happiness at having the opportunity to teach this course and to learn with the group.

Group Worship

For this session be prepared to lead with a short prayer asking for the Spirit's presence and blessing. These devotions should be given to volunteers who may choose a hymn verse, an appropriate passage of Scripture, a brief story, a short meditation, and/or a prayer. The devotion parts should relate to the lesson of the day. The teacher will be on the lookout for poems, clippings, quotes, and the like to put into the hands of volunteers. Ask for short devotions.

2. Explain the Course

After distributing the study text, state the purpose of the course and what it can do for each person in the class. Then ask pupils to page through the book and glance at the titles of the 12 chapters.

3. Introduction

Thinking of the Bible as "three books" is of course an attempt to look at its total content from a personal point of view. With the Spirit's help we find in every one of its many books elements of (1) instruction, (2) prayer and worship, and (3) guidance for living — toward God and toward man. You might wish to add that for the Christian reader every book has some relation to Christ or salvation history (even Ruth, Esther, Jonah).

The books of the Scripture have been called "love letters" (not only the epistles) addressed personally to us. Much of the Bible is indeed very personal. We can find ourselves in its sermons, characters, teachings, calls to repentance, and promises of grace. *It finds each one of us wherever we are, in all situations. In this sense it is an extremely human book.*

4. The Lesson

I. Taking God into Our Lives

Help your class personalize Col. 3:16-19 (read it in *Good News for Modern Man*, the new American Bible Society translation of 1966). Get opinions on the phrase "practicing God's presence."

Does God "color" our thoughts? control our actions? Or is He really "pushed out" of life, except for an hour on Sundays? Have you known couples of whom one lived "with God" while the other, though nominally "Christian," actually was a materialist? Is this a greater temptation today than 50 or 25 years ago? Introduce Ps. 10: 3-4. Is the modern generation "religious only in name and tradition"? or deeply Christian? How does routine Christianity and mere formal church membership destroy a "personal, practicing Christian faith"?

Similarly help your group dig deeper into the next concepts by looking closely at the related passages:

Poise — Eph. 1:18-20; the Spirit in a person — Eph. 3:16; then show that worship is related to "how we respect God" every day in everything we do (1 Cor. 10:31). Press home the point that no one can force himself into our hearts. The latch is on the inside! By the Spirit's power we open the door and let Christ come in!

II. How the Bible Helps Us

Show several devotional manuals and Bible reading lists to your class. Many persons have not yet discovered them. They are found in hymnbooks, some Bibles, church annuals, church periodicals, Bible Society leaflets, and Christian tracts (see references below).

Finding a paragraph or verse that especially strikes you (personally) is helpful. It not only "enlightens" you but serves as a guide or thought for the whole day. This proven technique needs to be practiced. Let your class discuss the meanings of Luke 17:33 (without reference to commentary in the lesson). What meaning does it convey? It is found six times in the gospels, and in various settings or contexts (Matt. 10:39; Luke 17:33; Matt. 16:25; Mark 8:35; Luke 9:24; John 12:25). "Life" or "soul" may be interpreted as "real, inner, self" (see Mark 8:35). How is this related to the voluntary "disciplines" of the Christian life? To Jesus' call to self-denial? (Matt. 10:24-25)

After this discussion you may wish to divide the class into small buzz groups of three, giving each group the task of finding a "thought for the day" in one of the paragraphs of James: chapter 1, vv. 2-4; 5-8; 9-11; 12-15; 16-18; 19-21; 22-25; 26-27.

Under "Help in Time of Need" ask three groups to examine and report on the cited passages dealing with (1) fear, (2) worry, and (3) death; or examine other passages listed under "Help in Time of Need" (study guide, p. 00). If time permits, ask: Which Bible passages have been especially helpful in your life?

III. Christ and His Word Sustain Us

After introducing the idea of "man is what he thinks," lead the class into the discussion and application of the key passage in each paragraph of part III: Luke 11:33-36; John 10:10; John 6:35.

5. Regarding Assignments

Motivate the use of the study text as a "skill book." Share thoughts from the introduction to this leaders manual. No class period will really be adequate for mastering the text. Request two readings of each chapter, one before class, another after the class period as a sort of review. This firms up new learnings. Refer to requirements of a high school course. Build up high personal resolve.

Similarly encourage each member of the group for the duration of the course to set aside time each day for the Bible readings. "No person can study the Bible for you. You alone must be the discoverer!" The readings will help the class get acquainted with many parts of Scripture. A skill course cannot be taught without personal experience.

Also show the personal value of such helps as the four lists at the end of the chapter, "Helps for Using Your Bible."

Read the next chapter of the leaders manual, and make several special assignments to selected individuals.

Two booklets by Elmer Kettner fit admirably into this sequence of two sessions on the devotional life. They might be assigned to two persons for home reading and report: *Living with My Lord* (especially Ch. 2) and *A Closer Walk with God* (especially Ch. 5).

6. Closing Thought or Prayer

Wrap up the session with a few summarizing sentences (highlights of the session), a "thought for the week" (section III of the chapter will suggest one), and a short prayer to the Holy Spirit "to guide us in our study and meditation."

As a different type of close you may wish to pass out slips of paper with these questions for each student to answer for himself:
1. In helping me grow spiritually I find the following to be most effective (number them in the order of their effectiveness in your own experience):
_____ Family worship
_____ Sunday worship
_____ Personal Bible use
_____ Group Bible discussion
2. In the light of this lesson, what changes in personal practices would you suggest to yourself?

References

Bible Reading Leaflets and Lists

American Bible Society, 1865 Broadway, New York, N. Y. 10023.

Canadian Bible Society, 1835 Yonge Street, Toronto 7, Ontario.

* Bringman, Dale S., and Frank W. Klos. *Prayer and the Devotional Life.* Philadelphia: Lutheran Church Press, 1964.

** Kettner, Elmer A. *A Closer Walk with God.* St. Louis: Concordia Publishing House, 1959. 95 pp.

** _____. *Living with My Lord.* St. Louis: Concordia Publishing House, 1961. 76 pp.

Sources of Bible Reading Lists:

The Lutheran Hymnal (pp. 161 ff.)

The Lutheran Annual

Portals of Prayer or similar devotional readings

(St. Louis: Concordia Publishing House)

** Young, Henry. *Bible Reading Guide* (Through the Bible in One Year). Minneapolis: Augsburg, 1958. 96 pp.

Chapter 2

The Bible and Your Devotional Life

Aim and Scope

In the previous session you have already introduced personal use of the Bible as a book of instruction in the Christian faith, as the chief resource for public, family, and private worship, and as the book to live by.

In this session you are to help your class get a clearer concept of meditation, not merely the theory but the practice. You will introduce several ways to encourage the individual to develop this art, using a procedure which may vary according to need and personal preference. You will want your students to *experience* meditation and learn that what the apostle Paul taught in all his letters is as vital and practical today as it was in his time.

Procedure

The method used should be determined by the outcomes desired. In this session you want everyone to experience or taste how rich God's Word is when we find its inner meaning for our lives. This will take practice. Several practice sessions are included. Take time for them, even if you must skip other sections or greatly condense them. The concepts are simple enough. Your task is to let students meditate in brief "quiet periods" and let a few of them report on their meditations. Draw out your students, to learn how many know what meditation as a process means. Share your own and the experience of other Christians as you follow your own lesson outline.

Teaching Outline

Introduction

Luther's experience
Meditation and modern Christians

18

I. *The Art of Meditation*
   Some definitions, Ps. 4:4; 19:14
   What is a Christian retreat?
   "Digesting the Word," Jer. 15:16
   Ps. 77; Joshua 1:8; Ps. 1:2
   Practice: the "I am" statements of our Lord (John's Gospel)

II. *Four Simple Steps*
   Approach
   Inquiry
   Prayer
   Action
   Practice passages (study book)

III. *Getting Started*
   The disciplines of the life "in Christ"
   God at work in us by means of His Word
   Spiritual food gives spiritual energy
   Every Christian can learn it
   Testimonies of people who have learned
   Modern man needs inner reserves

Overview of the Session

1. Opening worship
2. Reports on weekday study and meditation
3. Introducing the lesson
4. The three divisions of the lesson
5. Motivate assignments
6. Devotional close

Teaching the Lesson

1. Opening Worship

For your opening worship select a particularly striking short devotion you have used. A retreat experience may suggest your subject. It might be from a devotional booklet. It should reflect meditation *on* the text, not talk *about* the text. Particularly fitting

19

would be one chosen from *Hope for Today* (Marguerite Connell). Each devotion is composed of related Scripture passages without commentary.

2. Reports on Weekday Study and Meditation

Make the report session a sharing of meditation experiences students had in the past week. Also give opportunity to report problems and ask questions. List reported problems on the blackboard. At the close of the lesson ask the class if some solutions for these problems have been found.

3. Introducing the Lesson

You will find a translation of Luther's message to Peter the barber in Doberstein's *Minister's Prayer Book* (pp. 437 – 464). Many pastors have this. Cite similar examples of great leaders and their devotional practices (England's William Gladstone, John Bunyan, etc.). Then cite examples of people in our day from stories or books you have read. Add to them from your own personal or family experience. Some of the world's greatest leaders attribute their spiritual stamina and courage to meditation and prayer.

Assemble from your own or your pastor's library some devotional classics of the past and of today. See reference list in study book. Give your group a taste of the devotional life by reading several stanzas of Bernard of Clairvaux's hymns (p. 21). Show and describe these classics and several types of more recent date. Show how these books relate meditation to Christian living and action. They will supply many additional illustrations for the lesson.

4. The Lesson

I. The Art of Meditation

Check those paragraphs in the study book which give the gist of this section. Choose the similes or illustrations you want to use. But let your class develop them in discussion. The class should be in conversation with you throughout the lesson. The student must make discoveries for himself. Let the class explain the illustrations, for example, comparison to the assimilation of blood sugar through the body's circulatory system.

The entire class should discover the words used to describe meditation in the verses of Psalm 77. Get reports from those class members who have studied the lesson in advance. If this has not been done, assign the four passages to groups of three and get reports.

Each member of the class (privately) then takes one of the seven "I am" passages (assign, if necessary). Allow 5 minutes for meditation. Ask two or three to report their thoughts.

II. Four Simple Steps

This section may be taught on the basis of reports from four class members who received an assignment the week before. Each explains why "this step" is important, shows how one uses this approach or step, and relates how he or she has practiced it. The leader supplements where necessary.

The *approach* puts us in the right mood. It helps us put other things out of mind and open eyes and heart to the Word of God. This takes only a few moments. A one-sentence prayer will serve this purpose. Many Scripture passages are appropriate. Psalms 19 and 119 contain many such versicles for a devotional opening. We may develop readiness in a number of ways. Ask your class.

All Scripture is profitable (2 Tim. 3:16; Rom. 15:4). Every Scripture has some message. We must discern what kind of message it is and let it speak to us personally. It is in the asking of these questions (Is it instruction? warning? promise? etc.) that the worshiper gets at meanings and personalizes the verse or paragraph. Such *inquiry* is basic.

The Word of God to you requires a word from you to God. This is true encounter. The Word given requires our response, just as every question asks for an answer. This is best done in silent, personal *prayer*. Bible reading and prayer are two sides of one coin, just as in all worship we find the sacramental (God gives) and the sacrificial (we give).

It is step four *(action)* that you should especially explore with your class. The whole Book of James emphasizes this point (faith or confession without works is dead). The Word of God "should walk down the street" *in you!*

21

Again take time for the practice during the class period, even if part three must be slighted.

III. Getting Started

This is to supply the motivation. Why not begin with the last paragraph (modern man)? Start where your class members are. Do they think this practice is impossible? Why? Are the hindrances really insurmountable? Why does man need this more now than in the days when whole nations were Christian? What are the inner reserves today's Christians need?

The testimonials in this section come from students who took a course on Devotional Bible Reading. This is a good place to mention the fact that when Christians share their thoughts, privately or in a group, they help others meditate. We must "internalize" the Word before we can "externalize" it.

Bernard of Clairvaux gave us the hymn "O Sacred Head, Now Wounded." Other hymn stanzas attributed to Bernard illustrate the fruits of a Christian's meditation. Our hymnals have many such.

a. Jesus, Thou Joy of loving hearts!
　　Thou Fount of life! Thou Light of men!
　From the best bliss that earth imparts,
　　We turn unfilled to Thee again.

　O Jesus, ever with us stay;
　　Make all our moments calm and bright;
　Chase the dark night of sin away,
　　Shed o'er the world Thy holy light!

b. Jesus, the very thought of Thee
　　With sweetness fills the breast;
　But sweeter far Thy face to see
　　And in Thy presence rest.

　Nor voice can sing, nor heart can frame,
　　Nor can the memory find
　A sweeter sound than Thy blest name,
　　O Saviour of mankind!

5. Assignments

Scan through the next chapter of this leaders manual and select a few assignments which members of the class can handle. Get reports on daily readings from one or two persons. Reinforce the motivation given in the first session on "learning by doing." If necessary, comment briefly on the daily readings of the coming week. Get a show of hands on readings of the study chapter (before class? after class? both?).

6. Devotional Close

Use one or two stanzas of the hymns above as a basis for a short paraphrase adapted to the class as a closing prayer thought for the week. Look about for persons in the group who can be called on for closing prayers.

References

** Connell, Marguerite. *Hope for Today.* Chicago: Moody Bible Institute, 1965. 47 pp. Scripture selections.

* Doberstein, J. W. *Minister's Prayer Book.* Philadelphia: Fortress Press, 1959. 492 pp. $4.50.

* Kleinhans, T. J. *Alone with God.* Devotions from Martin Luther. St. Louis: Concordia Publishing House, 1962. 104 pp. $2.50.

** Kretzmann, O. P. *The Road Back to God.* St. Louis: Concordia Publishing House, 1935. $2.50.

Steere, Douglas V., and J. Minton Batten, eds. *The Very Thought of Thee.* Nashville: The Upper Room, 1953. 87 pp. Paperback. Selections from devotional writings.

Thomas, G. Ernst. *The Holy Habits of the Spiritual Life.* Nashville: Tidings, 1951. 63 pp. Paperback.

** Youngdahl, R. K. *Live Today.* Philadelphia: Fortress Press, 1959. 366 pp. $4.00.

Chapter 3

How to Read the Bible

Aim and Scope

We must admit that many church members have not received specific guidance and practical help for reading the Bible. Admittance into the church is by a short doctrinal course, in most instances by use of a catechism or by a simple review of Christian teachings and confession of faith. **Many admonitions to read and study the Bible are sounded from the pulpit, but who has given the practical steps for profitable, rewarding reading? To help people at this point is the aim of this session.**

But more than direction and know-how are needed. Most important is developing a desire, influencing the will, even touching the emotions. For that reason, supplying Christian motives is a second aim of the lesson. The stories of what the Bible has done for people in the past and is still doing today are therefore included. This lesson is to supply incentives for the regular use of the Scripture.

The task is not easily achieved when we think of the many hindrances put in the way by the materialism of our day. Consider also the fact that radio and television "do the reading" for many people and become allies of a life of ease that resists the putting forth of personal effort. Ask yourself and your class: Why is achieving regular Bible reading so difficult? What force alone can change that? It is the Holy Spirit at work in our hearts. Remember, He *does live* in Christ's people today as He has in every age.

Another way to open up discussion is to ask for a show of hands on such questions as:

1. How many have more than one version of the Bible or New Testament:

    KJV? RSV? Phillips? NEB? Other?

2. Have you ever read a book or taken a course on How to Read the Bible?

3. What is your present use of the Bible:
   in family devotions?
   in lesson preparation?
   in class use of Bible?
   chapter-a-day plan?
   listening to readings and sermons in church?

Procedure

Put the outline (see below) of the lesson on the chalkboard, and let the class fill in the details for each subpoint from their own advance reading of the lesson and from experience. Do not readily accept the "pious" and "wishful" answers. Test them with probing questions.

Be selective in choosing the points to be discovered and discussed in the class. Keep time limitations in mind. Expect the class to reread the lesson at home. From the additional incidents and materials supplied in the study book, choose what will help your class most.

Teaching Outline

Introduction

Bible use by Jesus and the apostles
Bible reading and the Reformation
The Book has influenced more lives than any other

I. *Why Read the Bible?*

The experience of Clarence Smith
Means to a new life and spiritual growth (eight references)
Psalm 119 on use of God's Word
The Bible and modern man

II. *How to Read the Bible*

By units of thought
Various kinds and purposes of reading
Clues to reading
New translations help

Where begin? Luke and Acts
The Psalms
Put yourself in the scene

III. *A Reading Plan*

Various plans
Testimony of modern readers

IV. *Time to Read*

The "disciplines" of the Christian life
Half the books take less than 45 minutes
Having the right motive and interest — the key
Sermons are no substitute
Learning to feed yourself

Overview of the Session

1. Opening worship: Acts 18:24-26
2. Reports and observations on homework
3. Introduction to the lesson
4. The lesson (parts I to IV)
5. Assignments
6. Closing summary and a sentence prayer

Teaching the Lesson

1. Opening Worship

Ask a member to read Acts 18:24-26, to make a few comments, and to say the opening prayer.

2. Reports and Observation on Homework

Take time to get one or two brief reports on the readings and meditations on Philippians. Encourage every member to start and keep to a daily schedule of reading. State again the necessity of practicing the Christian life (compare to skating, swimming, etc.). Give opportunity for questions on Chapter 3 of the study book.

3. Introduction to the Lesson

Our Lord's use of Old Testament Scripture is apparent throughout the gospels. There are 17 references in Matthew to the phrase "that it might be fulfilled." When people came to Jesus with a question, He frequently referred them to what they had read. (Note the following incidents: Matt. 12:3, 5; 19:4; 21:16, 42; 22:31.)

It was the conviction of the church in the first centuries of the Christian era that all men should become acquainted personally with the Scriptures as the great "public book of Christendom." Irenaeus taught that "the Holy Scriptures must be read by each for himself if he would advance in the Christian life." In the reading of the Scripture "a man has God Himself for teacher," said Barnabas. The Sacred Scriptures were in the homes, hands, and hearts of adults and children at an early date. Each Christian was expected to be as well acquainted with the Bible as the artisan was acquainted with his tools (Chrysostom). It is still through the personal use of the Scriptures that people today become "convinced Christians." (Source: Adolf Harnack, *Bible Readings in the Early Church*)

Call special attention to the role of the Bible in the life of Luther and in Reformation history. The report and literature of the Bible Societies of the world are full of remarkable testimony to the converting power of the Scriptures.

In Chile, South America, a man named Quiroga, walking along the seashore, came upon a few pages of a book among the debris washed up on the beach. He picked up the pages, spread them out, and dried them in the sun. Then he sat down and tried to read them. He found they contained the strangest message he had ever come across. He became fascinated by what he found, took the pages home, and showed them to a friend. The latter suggested they might come from the Bible, which he had heard a missionary speaking about. Quiroga tracked down the missionary, showed him his precious pages, and came away with a complete Bible under his arm. The Holy Spirit soon did His work through this book, and Quiroga not only became a Christian but dedicated himself for the rest of his life to distributing the Scriptures. (A. M. Chirgwin, *The Bible in World Evangelism*)

4. The Lesson

I. Why Read the Bible?

Do you have a Clarence Smith in your class? If you do, let him tell his own story. Call on the class to find reasons for Bible reading in the passages referred to in the next paragraph of the study text (Matt. 4:4; etc.). Take time to discuss these, then locate the verbs in Psalm 119 which testify to the Word's power to give spiritual life. Deal especially with the question: Is the Bible also for modern man? List on the chalkboard some of man's current problems: depersonalization in a world of automation, the frustrations of life, the search for purpose, moral degeneration in an "enlightened age," increase in mental illness, etc. Then ask: Why is the Gospel the only hope for modern man?

II. How to Read the Bible

Help the class discover the paragraphs in John 1 and title or name each paragraph. This will be more effective than just talking about making the paragraph basic. Our versification of Scripture is in many places a disservice to effective reading and has led to faulty reading habits.

Show a number of Bible editions that give the reader chapter and paragraph subtitles and other helps. Invite class members to examine them before and after class periods. Such editions are:

1. King James Version, Reference Edition, 1962. American Bible Society.
2. Concordia Reference Bible (KJV or RSV) with new concordance and Bible dictionary.
3. Revised Standard Version, wide-margin reference edition. Thomas Nelson & Sons.
4. The New Testament in Modern English, J. B. Phillips. Macmillan.
5. Today's English Version (*Good News for Modern Man*, New Testament. American Bible Society, 1967).

Ask questions on the points made in the study text on "various kinds of reading" and "different purposes." This section should help define "meaningful, intelligent" reading of the Bible. Ask for examples from the experience of class members.

Use the five different translations of Rom. 1:17 in the study text to show the value of modern translations. They are necessary for several reasons: (1) Language changes. *The Bible Word Book* by Bridges and Weigle contains articles on 827 words in the King James Version which have been affected by changing English usage since 1611, when the King James Version was prepared. (2) We now have more reliable Hebrew and Greek manuscripts on which to base a translation. We have a better understanding of New Testament times and of the translators' task. We do a disservice to youth if we give them "religion" in an obsolescent language that no longer speaks to the modern age. For another example, show the directness and clarity of Rom. 12:1-2 in (a) Revised Standard Version, (b) Phillips, and (c) New English Bible as compared with the King James Version text. Which would high school youth understand best? By reducing the time used in defining words we get more time to "teach religion!" Show a copy of *Good News for Modern Man*, the American Bible Society's New Testament (35¢), and point to its paragraph subtitles and line drawings. Prepare your lesson with this translation, to be able to speak from experience. For your own preparation get a copy of Bratcher's *Why So Many Bibles?* — a masterpiece of condensation (25¢).

This course suggests Luke and Acts as the first books for the beginning Bible reader. Get a copy of *The Inside Story* (American Bible Society, 35¢) to show the class. In what sense do Luke, Acts, John, and Romans really give "the inside story" of Christianity?

Help the class find the key word of Hebrews 11 ("faith"), of Philippians ("joy"), of John 13 and 1 Cor. 13 ("love").

III. A Reading Plan

Each year a congregation has several special opportunities to cultivate Bible reading. The stimulus can be a Bible-reading survey taken with the assembled congregation, a special Bible Sunday, or congregation-wide promotion of one of the many Bible-reading plans.

One of our pastors writes: "We have found that a Bible-reading program, like any other Christian project, needs (1) purposeful and prayerful action, (2) responsible and sustaining leadership, (3) something different and new from time to time, in terms of new reading assignments or new people bringing in new enthusiasm, and (4) an accounting and evaluation that help chart the progress of the program. Above all, it takes a humble but resolute faith in Jesus Christ, together with a devoted desire to serve in the name of the Christ, who exclaimed: "Blessed are those who hear the Word of God and keep it." (Luke 11:28)

IV. Time to Read

Is time really the thing that is lacking? Let the class "puncture" this common excuse. Then point out that every one of us actually can find several periods each day for reading. Is the solution in the concept of "discipleship"?

Other incentives for reading the Bible are:
* Personal Bible reading is essential for vital Christianity.
* Firsthand knowledge of the Bible is necessary for conviction.
* History shows that a church can go no farther
  than the insights of its people and that
  its power is closely related to a Bible-reading laity.

5. Assignments

Read the leaders manual for teaching the next chapter. Select the procedures you would like to use. Choose one or two assignments to make to individuals. Give your class a preview of what to expect. Raise their anticipation for presession reading of the next chapter. Invite individual testimonials on "how this chapter helped me." Stimulate morale for the daily readings by citing one example of what is in store for the reader who "listens" for God's message.

6. Closing Summary and Prayer

You can thank God for what He has given — for the enrichment, new understandings, and new skills you and the class acquired. Pray for the enlightenment only the Holy Spirit can give.

References

American Bible Society Tracts: "Why Read the Bible?" "How to Read Your Bible," "Personal Bible Reading." $2.00 per 100.

* Beegle, D. M. *God's Word into English*. Grand Rapids: Wm. B. Eerdmans, rev. 1964. 230 pp. Paperback. Careful investigation of modern translations. $2.25.

** Bratcher, R. G. *Good News for Modern Man. The New Testament in Today's English Version*. New York: American Bible Society, 1966. 600 pp. Paperback. $ .35.

** _____. *Why So Many Bibles?* (available from Concordia Publishing House). 44 pp. Brief but scholarly evaluation of modern English translations. $ .25.

* Bridges, Ronald, and L. A. Weigle. *The Bible Word Book*. New York: Thomas Nelson & Sons, 1960. 422 pp. $5.00.

Chirgwin, A. M. *The Bible in World Evangelism*. New York: Friendship Press, 1954. 166 pp. Paperback.

Harnack, Adolf. *Bible Reading in the Early Church*. New York: G. P. Putnam's Sons, 1912. Crown Theological Library.

Inside Story, The. Luke, John, Acts, Romans in the J. B. Phillips translation with modern pictures. New York: American Bible Society. $ .35.

** Love, J. P. *How to Read the Bible*. New York: Macmillan, rev. 1959. $3.95.

Reference Edition, American Bible Society's King James Version. New York: American Bible Society, 1962. (KJ053) $1.75. Contains alternative readings and list of over 500 words that have changed meaning since 1611.

** Young, Henry. *Bible Reading Guide*. Minneapolis: Augsburg, 1958. 96 pp.

Chapter 4

How to Study the Bible

Aim and Scope

Having helped your class discover for themselves some guideposts for reading the Bible with greater profit, you are ready to lead them into more serious Bible *study*. The mountain climber moves easily up the more gentle slopes of the peak he wants to conquer. He is soon faced with the sharper inclines as he nears the top. At certain points he must find fingerholds and toeholds for each new step. This lesson should help provide such fingerholds for Bible study.

More particularly, you will want four things to happen in your students: **(1) that they may begin to get excited about Bible study as "crossing the bridge from the world of the Bible to the world of today," or, to put it another way, "as we study the Scriptures Christ can give more meaning to all of life"; (2) that Bible study should not be an end in itself but a means to *functional Christianity,* to the fulfillment of our mission, to the expression of our priesthood, to effective churchmanship; (3) that class members learn the procedures of seeing wholes instead of mere pieces of a book in the three readings (this is vital for study); and (4) that your students begin to operate with the three basic questions: What does it say? What does it mean? What does it mean to me?** If you can develop inquiring persons, you have helped people to purposeful, rewarding study.

Procedure

How can these concepts "be experienced"? By involving the class in discussion. Let the members "fill in" the lesson outline which you place on the chalkboard, suggesting additional or alternate reasons and motivation for study (Introduction), showing the relation between Bible study and living (part I), relating their own study procedures or experiences (part II), and asking: What questions must the student ask of the text? (part III). With such a process the class actively gets a learning experience. This allows for creative teaching-learning.

Teaching Outline

Introduction

>New evidences of interest in Bible study
>The difference between reading and study
>What really is Bible study?
>Why should we study the Bible?

I. The Functions of Bible Study

>As related to our worship life
>To our witness to the world
>To personal spiritual growth
>To our family
>To "churchmanship"
>To faith and practice
>To a Christian world view
>To my mission in life

II. Procedures in Bible Study

>Why the college student first learns *how* to study chemistry
>Getting an overview
>Finding the outline
>Making it your own
>Increasing our working capital

III. Three Basic Questions

>What does it say? — Observation
>What does it mean? — Interpretation
>What does it mean to me? — Application

Give the study text several careful readings. Mark the points you would like to make. Write in your own illustrations. The best preparation is actually to choose a short book of the New Testament (for instance, Colossians), reading it three times and putting down new impressions gained with each reading. Note the time consumed and the personal benefits you gained. This will permit you to speak from a fresh experience. A skill is learned by doing.

Overview of the Session

1. Opening worship
2. Conversation with the class on the preceding session
3. Introduce the new lesson
4. Lead the class through the three-point lesson
5. Give assignments with motivation
6. Close with the Collect on Bible use

Teaching the Lesson

1. Opening Worship

Tie it closely to your purpose.

2. Conversation with the Class on the Preceding Session

Give class a chance to ask questions and share observations on homework assignments. You will get reports if they are assigned a week in advance.

3. Introducing the Lesson

You can do this in a number of ways. How account for a new interest in Bible study? Show a picture or book of the Dead Sea Scrolls. Note the fact that the Isaiah manuscript found at Qumran is practically identical with what we have in our Bibles. If you have saved a magazine issue or article devoting a great deal of attention to the Bible, exhibit it. Ask the class for evidences they have observed. Be sure to refer to the revival of Bible study in the Roman Catholic Church. Cite an instance from your own community.

Help the class distinguish between mere reading and purposeful study. Reserve enough time to get answers to "what really is Bible study?" How does the Catechism (deductive) help us understand the Bible? How may it be a hindrance to inductive study of the Scriptures? How many of us are really Bible students? Get reactions to the definition of Bible study as "crossing the bridge from the world of the Bible to the world of today." How is this meant?

4. The Lesson

I. The Functions of Bible Study

The purpose in this section is to relate Bible use to life, specifically to the mission of every Christian. You can use your time for this section in several ways. You might begin with a blank chalkboard and pose only the question: Why do we study the Bible? Let the class suggest various answers. Then ask them to select the four or five chief reasons. The class may actually supply most of the points made in the study text (without having read it). Or you could proceed by having individuals read the passages cited under the first seven points and draw the reason out of the texts. Or you may show the relation to the functions indicated in part I. Will everyone admit that each function is a valid Christian function? Drive home these points with an exploration of the actual place of Bible study in our own personal lives. *Keep the Christocentric use of Scripture in the foreground; not a moralistic, legalistic, or pietistic use.*

II. Procedures in Bible Study

Is there any value to courses on rapid reading? to high school and college bookstore guidelines on "How to Study Chemistry"? Since the Holy Spirit is our real teacher, does a lesson on "How to Study the Bible" have a place? Point out that the Bible was written in human language by human beings who followed the accepted rules of grammar and used concepts people can understand. (Would we profit from a course in Shakespeare?)

You may start this section functionally by having the class look at the structure of Luke-Acts. Point to the value of proceeding according to the built-in organization of Luke and Acts. Bible study involves the orderly processes of *overview* (to get the feel, taste, tone, direction, thrust) and *outline* (to get the direction, progression, development, movement toward climax). Follow these two steps by giving a book a distinctive title according to content, for the Book of Acts, for instance, "The Continued Acts of Jesus in His Disciples." Ask the class to give a distinctive title to the Gospel According to

Luke (for instance, "The Evangelist's Gospel"). Study also and especially involves that you "make it your own." The Bible was written for *our* instruction (Rom. 15:4). Using Acts as an example, suggest that the real message *(kerygma)* of the New Testament comes through very clearly in such a passage as Acts 10:34-43. Many more such recitals of the Gospel can be found by the student. Personal identification with our Christian mission in our world is the goal of studying Acts. Illustrate how key words help. (See Alvin Bell, *The Gist of the Bible*, Zondervan, 1961, for a fine demonstration of the help key words give in unlocking Bible books.) You may summarize this section under the question: What is your spiritual working capital?

III. Three Basic Questions

The first deals with *observation.* Select a short verse (for instance John 3:16 or 1 John 1:7), ask all members to read it carefully, and then ask for reports on what they saw. Put findings on chalkboard. A great biologist asked a student to examine a fish. He was not satisfied until the student had filled page after page with observations, including structure, symmetry, function of all moving parts, even counting the scales on both sides of the fish. The professor reviewing the student's observations said: "Now you have learned the first and most important lesson in becoming a scientist."

The second basic question pertains to *interpretation.* After having observed what is stated in a given passage, we ask: What does it mean? Not only the immediate text but also the context surrounding it conveys meaning. Looking up parallel passages is helpful. One must make sure, however, that these texts deal with the same subject, lest a foreign meaning be "imported" into the passage at hand.

Application brings us up to "here and now" and "you and me." But this third question must have two antecedents: questions 1 and 2. Point out the basic nature of these questions and how simple Bible study becomes when we operate with them. Again, illustrate with your verse-example.

Another and perhaps better way of teaching this section is to begin with a number of passages you have selected, giving one passage to each person in your class or to small groups (divide class into study cells). Briefly explain the three questions (three-step procedure). Ask each group to share its observations, interpretations, and applications in the cell. If time permits, ask one group to make a brief report to the whole class.

This will be excellent demonstration for the study assignments for the week.

Pacing your lesson is important. Expect the careful prelesson and postlesson reading of the study material at home as a standard requirement. It is not necessary to cover every paragraph or to add much commentary. The teacher's role is to point up the significance, to drive home the essentials, and to provide practical experiences. Return to the overview of this lesson and suggest to yourself the time you can spend on each section of the session.

5. Assignments

This may be the time to get a report on daily readings from every member of the class and to get testimonials on benefits received. Bible readings should never be just routine exercises. Are class members using the skills learned? Use the three questions: What does it say? What does it mean? What does it mean to me? Is meditation being practiced with approach, inquiry, prayer, and action? Is a new style of Christian living developing in persons? in their families? How much sharing of the course learnings has taken place? Are group members bringing others to class? Is new personal commitment developing? also a new concern for people?

Look at the next class session and make your assignments. Are you involving more members in making reports? Is the class beginning to feel more open and more like a community of believers?

6. Close with the Collect on Bible Use

"Blessed Lord, who hast caused all Holy Scriptures to be written for our learning, grant that we may in such wise hear them, read, mark, learn, and inwardly digest them, that by patience and comfort of Thy holy Word we may embrace, and ever hold fast, the blessed hope of everlasting life which Thou has given us in our Savior Jesus Christ." (*The Lutheran Hymnal*, p. 107)

References

** Bell, Alvin E. *The Gist of the Bible*. Grand Rapids: Zondervan, 1961.

** Halley, Henry H. *Bible Handbook*. Chicago: Moody Press. 968 pp.

Holman Study Bible RSV. Philadelphia: A. J. Holman Co., 1962.

** Manley, G. T. *The New Bible Handbook*. Chicago: Inter-Varsity, 1949. 465 pp.

* Wald, Oletta. *The Joy of Discovery*. Minneapolis: Banner Press, 1956.

Chapter 5

Studying the Bible with Others

Aim and Scope

Group Bible study can be one of the most rewarding experiences of a Christian's life. The tragedy is that so many persons have never experienced it. Many congregations fail to prepare people for and guide them into the joys of studying the Scriptures in a group. Too many church members as a result become "audiences" and "worshipers" but not "students." **This lesson is to help your class get a better understanding of the place of Bible study in the life of the Christian and to get a taste of it. To achieve this purpose, you as a leader are to guide the group into three experiences: (1) the "why" and "how" of group study, (2) the actual practice of the discovery-and-sharing method, and (3) doing the home assignment on Colossians. The joy of group study can be learned only by experience.**

Procedure

The class time will be wisely used if the leader after the opening moves quickly into the lesson and engages the class in discussion. Move through the introduction and part I. Describe the various methods. Allow enough time for practice study in small groups of four or five persons, using the simple Vaesteras method. This of course is only one of a number of approaches to group study, but it is quickly grasped and easily learned.

You may put your outline on the chalkboard and work through it with your class. When it is completed (by means of class discussion), it may look like the sample outline in this manual. Part I should be left blank until the class fills it in by discussion. The leader simply records the answers to the question: Why study the Bible in a class?

Teaching Outline

Introduction

"The only Bible you have is the Bible you know"
The experience of early Christians in study and prayer
The importance of discussion

I. *Why Study the Bible in a Class?*

It gets us into the Bible regularly
Stimulates personal discovery and thinking
Group participation and expression
Wider application to life
We learn better under a guide
We learn better with a definite course of study
(Examples: John's Gospel, Mark 10, etc.)

II. *Many Methods*

Following the textual units of a book
Starting with a situation or problem
Strengths and weaknesses of various methods
Type of course and goal determine method
Importance of freedom and participation

III. *The Vaesteras Method — An Example*

Description of Vaesteras method
Class practice in small groups
Importance of small study groups

IV. *Spiritually Productive Bible Study*

Ten criteria

Overview of the Session

1. Opening worship based on Acts 2:42
2. Reports on home study — exchange experiences
3. Introduction
4. The lesson
5. Homework assignment
6. Closing prayer based on 2 Tim. 2:15 RSV

Teaching the Lesson

1. Opening worship

Has your group advanced enough that class members can develop their own opening worship? How paraphrase Acts 2:42 for our congregation? What does it say to us? The prayer grows naturally out of this text for the people of God (all over the world) today.

2. Reports — Exchange of experiences

Has your class become frank enough to confess also some failures? to realistically deal with modern roadblocks to Bible use and study? Encourage this. Is your class still on "dress parade"?

3. Introduction

As an interesting illustration for "How big is your Bible?" take your Bible and hold it up by a few pages, then by a whole book (one of the gospels), then by a section covering Paul's letters, asking repeatedly, How big is *your* Bible? For a variation you may speak of the Old Testament canon and the New Testament canon. Explain that the church finally "accepted" the 27 books of the New Testament. Then ask: How big is *your* canon? That is to say: How many of the 27 books have you personally "received," "accepted," and now "made" a part of your life?

From the Biblical passages cited let the class draw some lessons on "group discussion and learning" and the role of dialog from the teaching of Jesus (Luke 24) and of the apostles (Acts 8).

4. The Lesson

I. Why Study the Bible in a Class?

Do not feed the answers to the class or call for what members have read in this section of the lesson; rather, ask the class to state the several advantages and reasons for a group approach to the Bible. Encourage them to give their own reasons, based on past class experience. Pose such questions as: How much studying of the Bible did you do before coming into our class? Is modern living conducive to serious Bible study? What stimuli do we get from one another? Explore the statement: "The Bible is bigger than any one person can grasp."

This may be the place to share the number and types of study occasions and study groups offered in your congregation during the course of a year and to name various courses of study offered in your youth and adult departments of the Sunday school and other study groups meeting during the week.

Cite an example from your own experience, like the two given in the study book (John; Mark 10). Or get "testimonials" from class members. You may ask: Which study course gave you the greatest benefits?

II. Many Methods

Whole chapters and books have been written on "How to Teach the Bible." The approaches vary, depending on (1) the lesson aim or goal. The method must help achieve the goal (the method for this lesson must include *experience*). The goal may include any combination of the following: getting knowledge (facts) or understanding (related to insights for living) or Christian attitudes and feelings or skills (abilities to do things, as gained by practice) or developing appreciation and interest (by exposure to people who have these). (2) Subject matter may determine the method (teaching history). (3) Abilities of class members must be taken into consideration. (4) The needs of persons in the class are another consideration in choosing a teaching-learning method.

Your task here is to simply show a variety of approaches to group Bible study. The study book greatly condenses this subject. The paragraph on "strengths and weaknesses" may give it in capsule form. Awaken anticipation for varied kinds of group Bible study and show that it can be exhilarating and stimulating.

III. Vaesteras Method—An Example

Give some insights. Awaken interest. Then give directions for use of the Vaesteras method, allowing no less than 15 minutes for group study experience. If possible, let at least one group report on its "questions, arrows, and candles." Each group should be given a different text for study.

The closing paragraph outlines the significance of neighborhood study groups which are being so effectively used in Europe and America. The pastor selects the leaders and gives them basic training by actually demonstrating small-group procedures. The church that can deploy its study groups into various communities served by the congregation has an important strategy for mission in the 20th and 21st centuries.

IV. Spiritually Productive Bible Study

These criteria may serve as a summary and close of this two-lesson unit: "How to Study the Bible" and "Why Study the Bible in a Class?"

The teacher may use them as part of the closing devotion, adding a one-sentence commentary to each point and closing with a short prayer. Or these statements may be revised into a litany. In that case a suitable response is made by the class to each point, for instance, this response to point 1: "Pour out on us, O Lord, Thy Holy Spirit." This should be prepared and mimeographed for class use.

5. The Study of Colossians 3 at Home

Show samples of various study guides provided by the church to acquaint the class with these resources and to awaken a desire to join some Bible study group when the courses in this series are completed. Many adults still think "Sunday school is for kids." They need to get a clearer image of Christian education as a lifelong process.

Explain that the homework materials on pages 59–62 of the study book are from a printed study guide which helps the student follow the inductive method, that is, makes him a discoverer in the Bible text itself. The assignment should be: Work this out for yourself at home, and be ready to share your findings at the next meeting of the class. Keep emphasizing the fact that reading the lesson at home before and after the class session is necessary to get the full benefits of this course.

6. Closing Verse and Prayer

For a more correct rendering of 2 Tim. 2:15 use the RSV. How much effort are we making? Are we rightly handling the Word of truth? This is what our course is all about.

References

** Coiner, Harry G. *Teaching the Word to Adults.* St. Louis: Concordia Publishing House, 1962. 129 pp.

* Colson, Howard P. *Preparing to Teach the Bible.* Nashville: Broadman, 1959. 150 pp.

** Feucht, O. E. *Bible Study in the Life of the Church.* St. Louis: Board of Parish Education (reprint of *Concordia Theological Monthly* article, July 1962).

** _____. *Small Bible Study Groups.* St. Louis: Concordia Publishing House, 1961. 13 pp.

Larson, Bruce. *Groups That Work.* Grand Rapids: Zondervan, 1967. 142 pp.

** Wald, Oletta. *The Joy of Discovery.* Minneapolis: Banner Press, 1956. 92 pp.

Filmstrip, for use if a second session is used for this lesson: "Teaching the Bible to Adults." St. Louis: Concordia Publishing House.

Chapter 6

Getting the Message of a Whole Book

Aim and Scope

This study course should provide both the basic concepts of the Christian's use of the Bible and a certain amount of practice or demonstration. This practice is to be provided through home study and class sessions. How much will be achieved will depend on the ability of the leader to provide experiences in the class session and to motivate and personally inspire class members to become students of the Bible.

This session is to help the study group see a book as a whole, "discovering" its outline, giving it a theme, and finding its meaning for the church of our day and for the individual Christian's mission in life.

For this purpose Paul's Letter to the Ephesians was chosen. It is not the simplest of the letters, but in content and scope one of the most important because it speaks about the church and its mission. It is directly related to continuing-education-for-service.

You could use 2 sessions or even 12 to study a book so rich in content. The goal is to help your class see the whole book in one session. *Overview, not detailed study, is intended here.*

Procedure

If the leader merely relates what he has discovered in the book, then it is he that becomes the learner and perhaps the lecturer, and the class members become observers and auditors. Do not yield to this "easy way out." Are there not better ways to achieve the session goal?

A second possibility would be to have the entire class give several readings to Ephesians before the session. The class members themselves may suggest titles for the book and for the main divisions and subdivisions, bringing their findings to the class. The leader then simply calls for reports from his diligent students and on the chalkboard records what they have reported. Various students will have different suggestions. Sometimes there will be debate as to what a section or paragraph actually treats. This is an ideal procedure. But it may take more than one class period.

A third possibility is that the leader puts only the five major divisions (as given in the study guide) on the chalkboard and lets the class give titles to the subdivisions. On the chalkboard he will merely show chapter and verse references of a subdivision, allowing space for the naming of each subsection. Below, by way of example, see two of the five sections.

Teaching Outline

(Example)   *The Church and Its Mission* (Ephesians)

1:1-2 _____ (salutation)

I. *1:3-23 God's Wonderful Plan (9-10) for You*

    3-6a _____

    6b-12 _____

    13-14 _____

    15-20a _____

    20b-23 _____

II. *2:1 – 3:13 The Gospel Transforms Us, Unites Us, and Equips the Church for Mission*

    2:1-10 _____

    2:11-18 _____

    2:19-22 _____

    3:1-13 _____

A fourth alternative is simply to have a copy of TEV *Good News for Modern Man* for each class member and read through the entire book in the class session. Read by paragraphs. Have members suggest paragraph titles and write them into margins. Leader queries to help class discover chief content, drawing on the study text which the class has read beforehand.

Overview of the Session

1. Opening worship (previously assigned)
2. Conversation and reports on Chapter 5 and reports on home study of Colossians 3
3. Introduce the new lesson
4. Lead the class through the Letter to the Ephesians
   (See notes on the Letter to the Ephesians in study text and leaders manual)
5. Give assignments and incentives for rereading Ephesians and finding additional insights
6. Close with a call to mission

Teaching the Lesson

1. Opening Worship

One of the hymns on the Word of God may serve as your opening. Follow it by a relevant prayer. Choose one or two stanzas. Are hymnals available? an accompanist? or will you sing a cappella?

2. Conversation and Reports

Time will not permit many reports. Choose some reports on *new* insights gained from Colossians 3. How does the whole chapter hang together? What is its message for us? our parish?

3. Introduction

The Epistle to the Ephesians provides striking insights into what it means to be a Christian, what the church really is, and how the Christian can equip himself for his mission in life. It has been called "the distilled essence of the Christian religion," "the spiritual constitution of the church," "the charter of Christian education." It gives the "noblest conception of Christian marriage."

4. The Lesson

I. God's Wonderful Plan for You, 1:1-23

Eph. 1:1-2. God's messenger speaks to God's separated people; the church united in Christ under grace.

47

3-14 — A hymn of praise for God's grace in Christ, with three stanzas, each closing with a refrain ("to the praise of His glory"): 6a, 12, 14. It is a doxology and "creed" praising election by the Father, redemption by the Son, sealing by the Holy Spirit (Rom. 8:16). Find in each stanza: Who? What? When? Where? Why? How? (Note: Time may allow doing this only for one stanza: vv. 3-6a.) How many times do you find the phrase "in Christ" or its equivalent? How vast is God's plan for us! The key: 1:9-10. What new image does this give you of yourself as a Christian? Summary: "All by grace; all in Christ!"

15-20a — Paul's prayer for a fuller knowledge of Christ, for wisdom, revelation, enlightenment (Is. 11:2), for the hope of their Christian calling, for the grasp of being God's inheritance, for resurrection power in their lives. Are we using this power?

20b-23 — Christ the Head of all things (of the whole universe, 1:9; of the church as His body on earth. See also 2:16; 4:4-6, 12, 16; 5:30.) The church is an organism. Christ the Head infuses His life into His members, His body. Church membership is Christ-membership. What is the relation between the church as organism and the church as organization or institution?

23 — The church is said to be "the fulness of Him who all in all is being fulfilled" (J. Armitage Robinson). No head is complete without a body, and vice versa. Christ is "completed" in His believing, working, witnessing, learning people. Read this section in TEV *(Good News for Modern Man.)*

II. *The Gospel Transforms Us, Unites Us, and Equips the Church for Mission, 2:1 — 3:13*

2:1-10 — The evidence of God's power in the church is shown by the spiritual resurrection (conversion) of sinners by God's grace. The new life in Christ is given them. By nature we are under the judgment of God. In conversion God raises us to a new life and to living in a heavenly "sphere" with Christ. Our transformation is a gift. Grace, faith, our new position, Christ Himself are all gifts! The grace we have received is to be expressed in a whole life of good works (v. 10). Why is this normal for everyone who is "in Christ"?

11-18 — Membership in Christ's body frees and unites. It erases all barriers, such as the wall of hostility between Jews and Gentiles.

Why was this wall of hatred so high then? How does Christianity remove barriers between races, peoples, and cultures today?

19-22 — These verses introduce three new pictures of the church. What are they? It is God's building. Who is the architect? Who are the workmen? What makes a congregation a habitation of the Spirit?

3:1-13 — This paragraph shows the unique and sublime mission of Paul, a messenger of grace to the Gentiles, and the mission of the church in the evangelization of the world. Why is this our greatest stewardship? We are Christ's "peace corps" today. How conscious are we of our mission?

III. How God Prepares Us for Our Mission, 3:14 — 4:16

3:14-21 — Paul's prayer for the spiritual growth of the church. Are we "four dimensional" in love? Note the educational significance of the verbs and nouns. What is your own spiritual pulse? (Help the class face up to this paragraph.)

4:1-6 — The mission of the church is fulfilled in her members. What is a life "worthy of our calling"? What four "human" qualities promote harmony? Why is love the prime requisite? Why does this take effort? Now list the seven divine factors of Christian unity (4-6). Who creates this unity? Why is our unity in Christ? Why not in our traditions or history? Why not in liturgies or church government?

4:7-16 — The mission of the church is to equip its members for ministry. Pastors and teachers are supplied *to prepare all God's people for the work of Christian service,* so that the whole church may grow to the maturity of Christ. *Pastor and people are in ministry together.* How does v. 12 give the solution to the church's manpower problem?

How do members equip each other for service according to vv. 12-16? What educational goals are suggested here? What teaching-learning process is pictured here? Who are both teachers and learners? How well are we equipping ourselves and one another for our mission?

IV. The Witness of the Church in Our Lives, 4:17 — 5:20

(As shown by four contrasts)
4:17-24   (1) *Give Up the Old Life — Put On the New*

What marks of pagan living are described here? How can we reveal "the image of God" to our generation?

4:25 – 5:2   (2) *Reject Heathen Vices – Cultivate Christian Attitudes*

Find the opposites of falsehood, anger, theft, evil talk, bitterness. Label one group of attitudes "ill will" and the other "good will" (31-32). What does it mean to give the Holy Spirit?

5:3-14   (3) *Flee Darkness – Walk in Light*

List the works of moral darkness mentioned (3-4). How can we expose darkness and let Christ be our light? (7-14)

5:15-20   (4) *Follow Christian Wisdom – Not Folly*

How do these verses emphasize witness by what we *are* and what we *do*? Paul turned his prison into a pulpit. In what sense is each of us in a pulpit every day? Eph. 4:1

V. *Living and Conquering in the Lord, 5:21 – 6:20*

(Our mission in four human relationships)

5:21-33   (1) *In the Marriage Relationship*

Find the parallels between the marriage relationship and our church relationship.

6:1-4   (2) *In Parent-Child Relationships*

What does "in the Lord" mean (6:1, 4)? Why does Christian nurture begin at home? What does this say to parents?

6:5-9   (3) *In Labor and Business Relationships*

How is the general principle stated again (vv. 5-9)? This was written in a master-slave society. Today we apply it to labor, management, business, the whole national economy. How does this give the Christian a higher view of his daily vocation?

6:10-17   (4) *In Christian Warfare* (Climax!)

Find the general principle in v. 10. What are the characteristics of the enemy we face? What belongs to the Christian's armaments? How can a congregation equip its soldiers "for their mission"?

6:18-20 – How do we keep in touch with our unseen Commander?

6:21-24 – Epilogue. Farewell: peace, love, faith, grace! Paul now sends his letter across the barrier of over 1,000 languages to all the world, to us, and through us to others. What shall we do with Ephesians? *Refashion our own lives and our congregations after this pattern.*

Ephesians calls for a church wide awake and in action. It asks us to walk worthily (ch. 4), live distinctively (ch. 5), stand courageously (ch. 6).

Preparing to Teach

One Bible scholar said he had read Ephesians every day for two weeks and that this book had become "his very own" since that time. There is no substitute for repeated reading. Follow the guidelines given in session VI for the three readings. Keep your own notebook. Read as a student. You will then be so "full of God's message in Ephesians" that your class will catch some of your own enthusiasm.

5. Assignment and Incentives

Class coverage in one session on Ephesians 1 — 6 must of course be sketchy. That is why the readings for the week give guidance for a second, more intensive reading.

6. The Closing: Call to Mission

Ask your class to follow you in their Bibles as you issue the call *to each member,* using the words of Is. 41:8-10, 13. Introduce this call with a few comments based on New Testament references to the Christian vocation. (Eph. 4:1; Phil. 3:14; 1 Peter 2:9-12)

> But you, Israel, My servant, Jacob, whom I have chosen, the offspring of Abraham, My friend; you whom I took from the ends of the earth and called from its farthest corners, saying to you, "You are My servant, I have chosen you and not cast you off"; fear not, for I am with you, be not dismayed, for I am your God; I will strengthen you, I will help you, I will uphold you with My victorious right hand. . . . For I, the Lord your God, hold your right hand; it is I who say to you, "Fear not, I will help you." (Is. 41:8-10, 13 RSV)

Tools

Appended to the study book chapter is a brief description of some basic tools for the lay Bible student. Help your class members build up their own Bible study library, adding a book each year. Bring these and similar books to several class sessions. Invite members to browse after class. Have the class secretary place orders for books members want. Get such a set into your parish library. For a fuller description of these and other books in the Bible study field see *A Treasury of Books for Bible Study*, by Wilbur M. Smith (W. A. Wilde Co., 1960, 289 pp.); *Multipurpose Tools for Bible Study*, by F. W. Danker (St. Louis: Concordia Publishing House, 1960, 289 pp.). Also consult Concordia Publishing House catalog. Throughout the course use some of these books in your teaching. Bring in for display Bible atlases and some of the books listed at the close of each lesson in this leaders manual. Encourage each class member to take home one book and browse through it.

References

** Blair, Edward P. *The Bible and You.* Nashville: Abingdon, 1953. Chs. 3 and 4.

* Bruce, F. F. *The Epistle to the Ephesians.* Westwood, N. J.: Revell, 1961.

Erdman, Charles R. *The Epistle of Paul to the Ephesians.* Philadelphia: Westminster, 1931. 130 pp.

Evans, William. *The Book Method of Bible Study.* Chicago: Moody, 1915.

Foulke, Francis. *The Epistle of Paul to the Ephesians.* Grand Rapids: Eerdmans, 1963.

** Hegland, Martin. *Getting Acquainted with the Bible.* Minneapolis: Augsburg, 1944. 239 pp.

* Hunter, A. M. *The Layman's Bible Commentary*, Vol. 22. Richmond: John Knox, 1959. Pp. 43 – 77.

* Robinson, J. Armitage. *St. Paul's Epistle to the Ephesians.* London: James Clarke & Co. Ltd.

Chapter 7

The Nature and Form of the Bible

TWO CLASS SESSIONS

Aim and Scope

The first chapters of the study text supply some skills for functional Bible use. But they do not provide all the background needed for a fuller understanding and overview of the Scriptures. In a time when textual and historical studies of the Bible are debated in church papers and secular magazines, the Christian needs more background. Chapter 7 tries to supply this. Each study group will need to determine which of the seven sections call for more class time and which need less. As group interests demand, the leader should supply more help in depth.

Each of the sections has a specific purpose already inherent in the subtitles. The leader may change each section title into a question, asking the class to pursue the question until it has a satisfactory answer.

The session aim is to help the group discover that:
1. **the Bible is a historical book, because God chose to reveal Himself in history;**
2. **the Bible does not take the form of a catechism supplying us with summary statements;**
3. **a closer look demands examining—**
   a. **revelation and Scripture**
   b. **Word and Scripture**
   c. **canonicity and authority;**
4. **the Bible is quite varied in form;**
5. **God has wonderfully provided for its inspiration, preservation, and translation;**
6. **it is available to all people;**
7. **it is a book of life and salvation.**

53

Planning Class Sessions

It will take two class meetings to cover the chapter to the satisfaction of the learner. For many group members you will be plowing over new ground. The outline which follows suggests approaches you may wish to use. The points are not always identical with the topic sentences of the study text. Many of them are put in question form to aid you in teaching. Be yourself. Put them in your words.

Teaching Outline for Two Sessions

Session One

Introduction

What skills did we learn? Chapters 1 — 6
How interpret the Bible; overview of Old and New Testaments. Chapters 7 — 12
Nature and form; human and divine. Chapter 7

I. *The Nature and Purpose of Scripture*

Revelation and record: what's the difference?
Why are nature, conscience, historical events not enough?
Why is the Bible unique?
God's self-revelation in Jesus Christ, Heb. 1:1-2

II. *The Bible and Inspiration*

The Bible, a human book
At the same time a divine book
Prophets and apostles — inspired recorders and interpreters
"Inspired": what does that mean?

III. *The Word of God and Scripture*

Use of the term "Word" in the Scriptures
The creative Word, Gospel, preached Word, written Word
God's Spirit works through God's Word

IV. *The Authority of Scripture*

Jesus used Old Testament as authority

Suppose we had no Bible?
"Only judge, rule, norm" of doctrine

Session Two

V. *The Form of the Bible*

A varied library
How are the books arranged in our Bibles?
How do the books differ in content and structure?
The imprint of many people and acts
Not a "catechism" but a "history"

VI. *The Canonical Scriptures*

Which books are authentic? ("Canon")
Grouping of Old Testament books (Hebrew canon – Ezra)
When and how were the New Testament books written?
accepted?
"Word of God" at time of writing
Who established the New Testament canon?
What about the Apocrypha?

VII. *Preservation and Translation*

No other book so carefully preserved
What do the Dead Sea Scrolls tell us?
How sure can we be of the Bible text?
Translations and variant readings
"Never off the presses"
The Bible "embraces the whole universe and all time!"

Overview of Each Session

1. Opening remarks to motivate alertness
2. Brief worship: a related Bible verse and prayer
3. Lead your class through those points chosen for a particular class session
4. Allow time for class questions at many points
5. Make assignments for the next session; motivate reading and study
6. Close with a brief prayer

Note: Detailed suggestions for each of the six items listed under "Overview of the Session" have been given for Chapters 1 to 6. With this background of experience each teacher-leader should have no difficulty in developing opening remarks and the opening and closing devotions.

By previewing the next session the new assignments can be selected and made in advance.

Each chapter in Part Two of the study book deserves two class sessions. It is more important that the leaders manual supply more background material for the teacher on these double-length chapters. For that reason the items for the session will continue to be listed, but details left to the planning of the leader.

How to Prepare for Your Class Sessions

Get a good grasp of the whole chapter. You can do this by a quick reading. Then go through the sections you will teach again, looking up the references. Underscore or write in the key words in the leaders manual or study book. Put down questions that occur to you for involving the class. Think how you will move logically and easily from point to point. Summarize the "learnings" at the close of each section.

For class use select only those Scripture verses that are needed to make a point. Select the clearest and strongest passages. How will you have them "discovered" by the class?

How Will You Teach the Lesson?

In such a way that the class participates from the very outset. This is determined by the method of the teacher. If he has the lesson "in hand" (meaning in mind and well outlined, with his procedures chosen), he will not need to lecture (except to give information which only he can supply). He can then develop meaningful conversation-type discussion and have the class members thinking, finding, reporting, and discussing each section of the lesson. Put your own personality and versatility into your plan. Be resourceful. The question in the lesson outline will open doors to discussion.

Further Suggestions for Teaching Each Section

Introduction

You may begin in various ways; for instance, by showing the relation of Chapters 1–6 to Chapters 7–12; or you may wish to begin with the following questions: What new learning did you get from this chapter? or: What is meant by the words "nature" and "form" in the title? or: What are some of the superficial and superstitious views people have of the Bible? or: How is the Bible very unlike a catechism? These should open up your group and make everyone a participant.

I. The Nature and Purpose of Scripture

In nature God speaks a universal language. He also does so through the human conscience, even to Gentiles (Rom. 2:14-15). God spoke directly to Noah, Abraham, Samuel, the prophets. But to preserve His messages (revelations) and pass them on to future generations, a written record was necessary. For a fuller treatment of revelation as related to Scripture, see Chapter 2 of *The Bible —Book of Faith* (Augsburg, 1964). Help your class discover the many things told us in Heb. 1:1-2.

II. The Bible and Inspiration

This section helps to explain why the Bible has such wide appeal, even to Hollywood moviemakers. No one can claim to be educated unless he is familiar with the Bible. It is indeed a very human book. No other book puts such a searchlight on man! Yet it is truly God's inspired Word. For this the Scripture has abundant evidence. The "thus saith the Lord" is built into it in many ways and many places. Our Lord's use of the Old Testament is the best proof. Help the class see all that is said in 1 Peter 1:10-12 and 2 Peter 1:16-20. The writers gave God's interpretation of events. Even the crucifixion of Christ could be considered only a martyr's death without the Scripture's interpretation.

Read a good recently written article in a Bible dictionary on the inspiration of the Bible. The writers in the Old Testament particularly mention sources — records or books — no longer extant. By way of example, see Num. 21:14; Joshua 10:13; 1 Chron. 29:29; etc. The genealogies were carefully recorded and handed down from generation to generation. We should not by rationalizing explain away either the divine factor or the human factor in God's plan to give us the Scriptures.

For a detailed account of sources used especially by the writers of Kings and Chronicles, read pages 255 — 258 of Bruce, *The Books and the Parchments*. Luther thought that Moses might have used Abraham's "Little Book" as a resource for Genesis (*Luther's Works*, Vol. 4, p. 308, Concordia, 1964). We should not rule out the use of extant sources by the inspired writers of the Bible.

III. The Word of God and Scripture

This may at first seem like a "tricky" section. A sharper examination of texts in their contexts suggests being more careful in our use of the term Word of God. One approach would be to select four or five passages, each of which uses the term Word in a slightly different sense. Allow enough time to look at each context. This can be part of a previously given assignment. Why must we distinguish between Christ the incarnate Word (the object of our faith) and the written Word (the medium for our faith)? Does the Bible save us, or does Christ?

IV. The Authority of Scripture

Drive home the point that without Scripture we have no sure and safe guide and are left to our own self-deceptions. Church bodies can err — and have erred! How do our creeds (Nicene) and confessions help us keep our faith solidly founded? Ask the class to find the phrase "according to the Scriptures" in the Nicene Creed (formulated A. D. 325, reaffirmed A. D. 381). Then have someone read the quotation from the Formula of Concord.

Why did the reformers and men like William Tyndale insist that the common man have a Bible and be free to read it by himself?

On the authority of the Old Testament no voice is stronger than that of our Lord Jesus Christ. Jesus accepted the Old Testament writings. This is very vital for our acceptance of them. These books constituted Christ's Bible. (See Matt. 15:3-4.)

One scholar very properly observes that Jesus accepted the Old Testament's history "as the preparation for Himself, and taught His disciples to find Him in it. He used it to justify His mission and to illuminate the mystery of His Cross. He drew from it many examples and most of the categories of His gospel. He reinforced the essence of its law. . . . [He] fed His own soul with its contents, and in the great crises of His life sustained Himself upon it as upon the living and sovereign Word of God." (George Adam Smith, *Modern Criticism and the Preaching of the Old Testament*, p. 11)

Session Two

V. The Form of the Bible

You might begin by asking: How does the Bible differ in form from a catechism? This will show that God didn't do all our thinking for us but provided the basic teachings in the framework of happenings in history which God interpreted for us.

The statement: "God did not give us a catechism," may surprise the reader. A catechism is a pedagogical aid often in question-and-answer form. It is a summary of teachings drawn from the Bible and is most helpful in teaching basic truths of Scripture. God has left such summaries and books of systematic theology to men. He chose to reveal Himself through history, in God-directed events, but events interpreted by Him through the prophets and apostles. The Bible is not simple. It is quite complex. Its form and nature will challenge us to the end of time to discover God's will as it relates to man's old and new needs and questions. No person can exhaust this well of living water.

The Bible is a collection of books of various kinds and structures. How does its great variety intrigue us? challenge us? its unity surprise us? How does its unity argue for "one divine Author"? With a time line drawn on the chalkboard, show approximately when the various writers lived. Have students turn to the charts on pages 171 – 176 of the study book.

VI. The Canonical Scriptures

To get additional background material, read an article on the Old and New Testament canons in a good Bible dictionary.

The arrangement of the books in the Old Testament, as we know it from our English Bible, is: (1) five books of the Law, or the Pentateuch (Genesis to Deuteronomy); (2) twelve books of history (Joshua to Esther); (3) five books of poetry (Job to Song of Solomon); and (4) seventeen books of prophecy (Isaiah to Malachi; the five Major and twelve Minor Prophets). This order we find in the Septuagint (Greek translation of the Old Testament, — ca. third century B. C.) and in the Vulgate (fourth century A. D.). An earlier arrangement into three major groups is referred to by Jesus in Luke 24:44, namely, (1) Law: Pentateuch, (2) Prophets: former prophets — Joshua to 2 Kings; latter prophets — Isaiah, Jeremiah, Ezekiel, and twelve minor prophets; (3) Writings: the five books of poetry, Esther, Daniel, Ezra-Nehemiah, 1 and 2 Chronicles. (Jesus evidently included all of these in the term psalms in Luke 24.)

Luke 11:30 is also significant in that it gives the "A to Z" of the Old Testament by referring to the blood of Abel in Genesis and to the blood of Zacharias in 2 Chronicles. The latter was the last Old Testament book in the earliest grouping of Old Testament books.

The Jewish historian Josephus (first century A. D.) writes: "We have not ten thousand books among us, disagreeing with and contradicting one another, but only 22 books which contain the records of all time and are justly believed to be divine." In checking the books he lists we find that they are identical with the 39 which we now have in the Old Testament. The number is not the same because such books as 1 and 2 Samuel are considered one book, and the 12 Minor Prophets likewise are considered only one. The number 22 was also used by Origen (A. D. 185 – 254) and by Jerome (A. D. 347 – 420). So the Old Testament of Jesus' day is the Old Testament we have in our day. Most historians indicate that this assembling of Old Testament books was completed by Ezra.

Most of the books of the New Testament were evidently collected by the middle of the second century and were accepted as an authentic record of the ministry of our Lord and the teaching of the apostles. The earliest collection included some books which were considered helpful but were later excluded from the New Testament canon, for instance, the Shepherd of Hermas and the Letter of Clement. There are also other early documents that are instructive, for instance, the Didache, written about A. D. 150 as a guidance manual for Baptism.

To introduce the Old Testament Apocrypha, show the class the English translation of 1957 (Thomas Nelson & Sons) or a German Bible or a Roman Catholic Bible with the Apocrypha included. Luther did not classify these books as canonical. Less familiar are the apocryphal books often associated with the New Testament. A sample story in one of these apocryphal books is this purported incident: When Jesus as a child made some little birds out of mud and then clapped His hands, the birds flew away. The Old Testament apocryphal books fall into four classifications: historical, religious fiction or legend, wisdom and ethical literature, prophetical and apocalyptic literature.

VII. Preservation and Translation

You may wish to begin with some facsimile photos of the great Biblical manuscripts (see large encyclopedias or Bible dictionaries) or pictures of some Dead Sea Scrolls. Consult articles in an up-to-date Bible dictionary (since 1960). Check your church and public libraries.

The scribes counted the number of characters on a page. If the count did not correspond with the text they were reproducing, the page was rejected. This is only one example of the utmost care taken by the copyists.

The Jewish rabbis had such high veneration for the text that when a copy of the Old Testament was worn out by use it was buried or put into a genizah (a storage room attached to the synagogue).

We have also the witness of some very old and important New Testament manuscripts. The Codex Sinaiticus (found in 1844 in a Mount Sinai cloister) and the Codex Vaticanus, so named because it is in the Vatican library, are both from the fourth century. The Washington Manuscript dates from the fourth or fifth century (now at the Smithsonian Institution). The Codex Alexandrinus was copied in the first half of the fifth or sixth century. The more recently discovered papyri include the Chester Beatty Papyrus (third century A. D.) and the Bodmer Papyrus (about A. D. 200). All bear witness to the accuracy of the accepted texts.

The division of the Bible into chapters and verses was not in the original manuscripts but was made much later. The division of each book into chapters did not come until A. D. 1244. The division into verses was made over a period of about 100 years and first appeared in both Testaments in a Latin Bible issued in 1555.* N. R. Lightfoot, on the flyleaf of his book *How We Got the Bible*, has three quotes to share with your class on the reliability of the Biblical text. God has spoken in Jesus Christ, and He still speaks to those who hear and read the Bible today. It is not a dead book but a living contemporary voice which we hear through the words of apostles and prophets. If we take seriously our doctrine of the means of grace, then we recognize that the Scripture is not merely an ancient deposit of divine truth but a vital channel through which the Spirit today reveals God and reclaims man. The Bible in fact authenticates itself as it demonstrates its power in our lives.

* "The Hebrew Old Testament was divided into verses by Rabbi Nathan in 1448 (first printed in a Venice edition of 1524). This division was adopted in the Latin Bible of Pagninus in 1528, with a different division in the N. T. The first Bible that has the present verse division in both Testaments is Stephanus's Vulgate of 1555." (Sir Frederic Kenyon, *The Story of the Bible*, p. 40.)

References

Blair, Edward P. *The Bible and You*. Nashville: Abingdon, 1953. 154 pp. (Ch. 1)

** Bruce, F. F. *The Books and the Parchments*. Westwood, N. J.: Revell, 1963. 288 pp. Excellent scholarship; recognized authority in the field.

Herklots, H. G. *How Our Bible Came to Us*. New York: Oxford University Press, 1954.

** *Introduction to the Bible*. Vol. 1 of *The Layman's Bible Commentary*. Foreman Kelly, Rhodes, Metzger, Miller. Richmond: John Knox Press, 1959.

Kenyon, Sir Frederic. *The Story of the Bible* (new edition by F. F. Bruce). Grand Rapids: Wm. B. Eerdmans, 1967. (Paperback)

** Lightfoot, Neil R. *How We Got the Bible*. Grand Rapids: Baker, 1965. 128 pp. A must for the teacher; suggest that class members purchase it also.

** Manley, G. T. *The New Bible Handbook*. Chicago: Inter-Varsity Fellowship, 1950.

"Revelation," Theo. S. Liefeldt, Ch. 2 in *The Bible: Book of Faith* (The American Lutheran Church). Minneapolis: Augsburg, 1964.

The American Bible Society's Film: *Our Bible — How It Came to Us*, Part I (30 minutes). An excellent review. Use in an extra session of class.

Chapter 8

Understanding the Bible

TWO CLASS SESSIONS

Aim and Scope

The 10 underlying factors of Biblical interpretation discussed in this chapter may also be regarded as presuppositions for understanding the Bible. For group discussion two sessions are needed: one for points 1 to 5, a second for points 6 to 10. If you note some repetition, it is to give the group repeated exposures in this comprehensive course. This chapter is followed by one dealing in detail with four basic interpretation principles.

The purpose of the sessions is (1) to help the student look at and think through 10 preliminary observations and recognize their relationship to personal use and interpretation of the diverse literature of the canonical Scriptures (most of these have been referred to and partially treated in earlier chapters); (2) to give opportunity to apply each point with one or two examples; (3) to set the stage for the four basic interpretation principles.

Process and Method

On the part of the student: Presession reading of the points assigned for the session; participation with questions and examples during each session; postclass review of what was learned; doing the home assignments.

On the part of the leader: Making your own outline after digesting the sections in the chapter; writing in the questions you would ask; selecting the illustrations and examples from your own Bible study and experience; pacing yourself so that each point receives enough attention to meet class interest.

Your procedure will depend partly on how much background your class has now acquired. Keep in constant conversation with your group. Try not to stymie their thinking and questions.

Teaching Outline for Two Sessions

Session One

Introduction

The Ethiopian's question (Acts 8:30)
It is being asked oftener than ever. Why?
The Holy Spirit our Teacher (John 14:26)
Christological interpretation (1 Peter 1:11)
Basic factors in understanding Scripture

I. *We Work with a Translation*

Which text is decisive? Why translations?
Are they reliable?

II. *God Speaks in Human Language*

Can we understand the infinite God?
God uses our thought forms and speech (anthropomorphic)

III. *The Bible Uses Various Literary Forms*

How many can you identify?
Hebrew poetry; prophecy through type and symbol
How is form related to understanding?

IV. *Time and Setting*

When? Where? Why? (time, circumstances)
Find the "then and there" meaning first
Archeology, history, customs, culture
Some examples

V. *The Bible Is an Unfolding Revelation*

No full-blown theology in any one book of the Bible
In what sense is the Bible an "unfolding revelation"?
Like a drama it unfolds, scene upon scene, to the climax

VI. *Keep Scripture's Specific Purpose in Mind*

Redemption taught from Genesis to Revelation
The proper scope of Scripture

VII. *The Bible Teaches Law and Gospel* (Sin and Grace)

Not just another book of religious ethics
Law and Gospel in Old Testament: Where? How?
New Testament: Where? How?
Relation to central teaching: justification by grace through
faith (Martin Luther's main principle)

VIII. *Christian Doctrine Must Be Based on Clear Passages*

Essential teachings clearly stated, many times
Teaching not to be based on passages "isolated" from context
What about obscure passages (variants)?
The Bible is both simple and complex

IX. *Don't Carry Your Meaning into Scripture*

Difference between exegesis and eisegesis
Becoming "discoverers" but not "inventors"
Damage done by opinionated, "positional" interpretation
Importance of the inductive approach

X. *The Christian Use of the Bible*

2 Tim. 3:15-17
Misuse by radical liberalism and by false literalism

Overview of Each Session

1. Opening worship. Readings from Luke 24:25-27 (session 1);
vv. 44-47 (session 2). Talk about Jesus' use of the Old Testament. The Christological understanding of the Bible is
indicated in Scripture itself.
2. Reports on home study assignments; questions
3. Introduction

4. The lesson
5. Assignments
6. Devotional close. Acts 8:26-40 (Session 1); Ps. 119:18 (Session 2).

Further Suggestions for Teaching Each Session

Session One

Introduction

Beginning with the Ethiopian's question, inquire why this question is being asked more frequently now. How did the many sects arise? Not only various denominations but such strange groups as Christian Scientists and Jehovah's Witnesses? Why so many different commentaries on the Bible?

Then point out that the Bible has influenced more people than any other book, that its chief message is understandable to all who will take time to read it. It is understandable when the reader approaches it in faith and is guided by the Holy Spirit. How does John 14:26 apply here? Yet even Luther said: "When I find a passage I don't fully understand, I take off my hat [in reverence] and go on to the next verse."

If in your opening worship you pointed out Christ's approach to the Old Testament, you may now ask the class: How did the apostles understand the Old Testament? How is 1 Peter 1:10-11 related to our quest?

Introduce the "basic factors" concept. Look up "prolegomena" in a good dictionary. The 10 points are preliminary steps to sound interpretation.

I. We Work with a Translation

Christian theologians have always insisted that sound doctrine must be based not on any translation but on the best Hebrew and Greek texts we have. The Dead Sea Scrolls proved the correctness of the received text of Isaiah. No two languages are so alike that there is always a word in the modern language whose precise meaning corresponds to the word in the Biblical text. There are now 75 extant English translations of the New Testament. One of

66

these is the American Bible Society's *Good News for Modern Man*. Translations are the work of expert linguists who distinguish between (1) object words (table), (2) event words (believe, came), (3) abstract words (red, black; the quality of something), and (4) relational words (righteousness). It was Dr. Francis Pieper who in his *Christliche Dogmatik* said that "among the generally accepted Bible translations not a one exists in which the Christian doctrine in all its parts is not clearly expressed." Roman Catholic and Protestant scholars have already agreed on a Revised Standard Version text and are now working toward a common Hebrew and Greek text. *The Bible Word Book* by Bridges and Weigle shows why language changes demand new versions.

II. God Speaks in Human Language

God used human writers, their manner of speech, their ways of telling a story. This is part of the human side of the Bible. The Bible is still so human and so relevant that people of every language find themselves identified in it. Yet no language is adequate to fully reveal the infinite God. How is the incarnation of Christ related to God communicating with man? In a good dictionary look up "anthropomorphic" and "anthropopathic" and note how they describe God's accommodation to man.

III. The Bible Uses Various Literary Forms

Choose several practical examples to show the relation of literary form to interpretation; for instance —
The parable of the Ten Virgins
The birth of Jesus
Several verses of Psalms (thought and rhythm)
Typological prophecy (the Passover)
Verses from Ephesians: 1:3-4 and 5:25
In addition to Psalms, Proverbs, and Ecclesiastes, which are largely poetical in form, there are poetic sections in 200 other chapters of the Bible. Why is poetry different?

IV. Time and Setting

Here is the place to introduce two significant phrases: "There and then" and "Here and now." Before we can determine meaning for ourselves today, we need to know what the passage meant at the time it was spoken or written. It is also important to know the place and circumstance of writing. A Bible dictionary or book on archeology will supply illustrations of old customs, for instance, threshing grain with oxen. See Manley's *The New Bible Handbook*, pp. 425 to 438, on geography and customs.

V. *The Bible Is an Unfolding Revelation*

Another term used for this aspect of the Bible is "unfolding revelation" (or "progressive" revelation, if rightly understood). This does not imply a human, evolutionistic development of doctrine. There is one God from Genesis to Revelation. In the course of time He unfolds His will toward men. An objective study of Scripture shows that God revealed Himself and His will more and more through a series of mighty acts and the writings of Moses and prophets. The types and symbols of the Old Testament may not have been fully understood by all the people. Their full significance comes through when we read the Book of Hebrews. Some laws and ordinances had outlived their purpose when Christ, the Fulfiller (Prophet, Priest, and King), had come and therefore were abrogated (Col. 2:16-17). This is the significance of the New Testament phrase "in the fullness of time." One of the best books to show the interrelatedness of the Old and the New Testament is Suzanne deDietrich's *God's Unfolding Purpose*. Like a great drama the Bible unfolds its message scene after scene until it reaches its climax in Christ's work of redemption.

Session Two

VI. *Keep Scripture's Specific Purpose in Mind*

Failing to keep God's specific purpose in mind, some have regarded the Scripture as a sort of general encyclopedia, a compendium of knowledge from many fields. This proposition of course is false, making of the Bible more than it is intended to be. Galileo made this point when he said: "The Bible was given not to tell us how the heavens go, but to tell us how to go to heaven." This is not to say that the Bible is subject to error when it touches on other fields. It is only to say that its specific purpose is to teach salvation in Christ.

Historical facts are reported in most Biblical books, for instance, in Samuel, Kings, and Chronicles. For similarities and differences see Ex. 20:8-12 and Deut. 5:12-16; Ex. 23:14-17 and Deut. 16:1-17. Archeology has verified hundreds of Biblical references. For instance, Solomon's copper mines were located on the basis of references in the Bible. Read an article on Biblical archeology in a good Bible dictionary.

VII. The Bible Teaches Law and Gospel

This may be termed the keystone of understanding and interpreting the Bible. Those who fail to recognize it confuse themselves and their students, making Law out of the Gospel and Gospel out of the Law. Fortunately, Christian theologians of many denominations are beginning to see this more clearly today. Both Galatians and the Letter of James have something to say to us on Law and Gospel and their use. (Read Ramm's treatment in *Protestant Biblical Interpretation*, p. 57.)

VIII. Christian Doctrine Must Be Based on Clear Passages

Your class may need no demonstration of this point. If a demonstration is necessary, follow either plan A or plan B. Plan A: divide into five small groups, each taking one set of passages: (1) sin, (2) grace (OT), (3) redemption (NT), (4) deity of Christ, and (5) the resurrection. Plan B: It may be more important to spend the time on obscure passages. Call attention to textual footnotes in RSV. There are thousands of variant readings, but the best scholars have asserted that they do *not* affect a single fundamental teaching of the Christian faith. Textual study is painstakingly careful. Some texts will perhaps remain obscure and always puzzle interpreters (for instance, 1 Cor. 15:29). We are to be responsible interpreters. (2 Tim. 2:15)

IX. Don't Carry Your Meaning into Scripture

Stress the inductive nature of genuine Bible study. We are not to come to the Bible with preconceived notions. Too many make Scripture the proving ground for their own theories. This has caused disharmony and divisions in the church. "Positional interpretation," which takes a man-made formula and then seeks proof from Scripture, is dangerous. *Exegesis* means explaining "out of" the Biblical text. *Eisegesis* means reading something "into" the text.

From your experience or observation cite examples and get some examples from the class.

X. The Christian Use of the Bible

Ask your class to take a closer look at 2 Tim. 3:15-17.

— "To instruct you for salvation through faith in Christ Jesus." John 20:30-31
— "Profitable for teaching": in all areas of doctrine and life. Ps. 119:105
— "For reproof": God's law keeps judging us and showing us our sins. Rom. 3:23; 7:7
— "For correction": for restoration and renewal by the Gospel. 2 Cor. 5:17
— "For training in righteousness": sure guide to a God-fearing life. Ps. 119:9-11
— "That the man of God may be complete, equipped for every good work."

The right use of Scripture leads to spiritual maturity and equips us for our mission in life. Eph. 4:11-12 (See Gaebelein's *The Christian Use of the Bible.*)

Liberalism in theology is a departure from the *sola Scriptura* principle. Having given up a serious view of inspiration, it develops theologies informed by the philosophies and theories of man.

False literalism fails to take into account the many literary forms of Scripture and the time and setting of writing (see points III and IV of this chapter). Example: Millennialistic groups fail to recognize that the sense intended by the Holy Spirit may be something quite different than the literal meaning. Their futuristic interpretations of the prophets, on the other hand, fail to take into account the "then and there" meaning. Call on the class to find the relevance of 2 Peter 3:15-18 and 2 Tim. 2:15 to a Christian use of the Bible.

References

Bridges, Ronald, and Luther A. Weigle. *The Bible Word Book*. New York: Thomas Nelson & Sons, 1960. 422 pp.

** Colson, Howard P. *Preparing to Teach the Bible*. Nashville: Convention Press, 1959. 148 pp.

** deDietrich, Suzanne. *God's Unfolding Purpose: A Guide to the Study of the Bible*. Philadelphia: Westminster Press, 1960. 287 pp.

Franzmann, Martin H. *The Word of the Lord Grows: A First Historical Introduction to the New Testament*. St. Louis: Concordia Publishing House, 1961. 324 pp.

Gaebelein, Frank E. *The Christian Use of the Bible*. Chicago: Moody Press, 1946. 119 pp. (out of print).

———. *Exploring the Bible*. New York: Harper & Bros., 1929. 214 pp. (out of print).

Johnson, Douglas. *The Christian and His Bible*. Grand Rapids, Mich.: Wm. B. Eerdmans, 1953. 144 pp. (paperback, rev. 1961).

** Manley, G. T. *The New Bible Handbook*. Chicago: Inter-Varsity Christian Fellowship, 1950. 465 pp.

** Ramm, Bernard. *Protestant Biblical Interpretation*. Natick, Mass.: W. A. Wilde Co., 1956. 274 pp.

Chapter 9

Basic Principles of Interpretation

TWO CLASS SESSIONS

Aim and Scope

You will again want to use two class sessions to deal with this chapter. Many church members have never read a book or taken a course on interpreting the Bible. Yet all of them have asked questions about the meaning of certain difficult Bible passages. The introduction and the first two sections in the first session and sections four to six in the second will provide two "full menus" for your class.

The purpose of these sessions is (1) to awaken new interest in sound Biblical interpretation; (2) to help your students understand four basic principles for interpreting the Scriptures and get some experience in their use; (3) to point out the richness of Scripture embodied in its figures of speech and how to find the meaning of various figurative forms; (4) to emphasize again that Christ is the key to unlock Scripture and its meaning; and (5) to close with an appeal for spiritual discernment, calling on the Holy Spirit, the Author of Scripture, to be also its Interpreter.

Process and Method

On the part of the student: Presession reading of the chapter section assigned; bringing to class questions related to the study text or problems in interpretation; postclass review of what was learned; doing home assignments; developing one's own notebook.

On the part of the leader: Select the facts, questions, examples, and procedures you will use in class after digesting the study text sections to be covered; pacing your progress and choosing major points for the best use of class time.

Bernard Ramm's book, *Protestant Biblical Interpretation,* is one of the most helpful in this area. There will be references to it at several points in these notes. Most Biblical scholars are agreed on the basic principles. The historical-critical school of interpretation has questioned some of the old principles. Biblical interpretation suffers today because speculative theologians like Rudolf Bultmann and Karl Barth adopted certain philosophical theories as presuppositions. It suffers also at the hands of those who question the historicity of the Old and New Testaments. These theories have led to much confusion.

The Christian teacher is on safe ground when he accepts God's own testimony inherent in the Scripture. While other religions of the world are based on philosophies born in the minds of men, the Christian religion is a revelation of God through His actions in history, such as the birth, life, death, and resurrection of His Son, Jesus Christ. This "rootedness in history" we have seen throughout this course.

Teaching Outline for Two Sessions

Session One

Introduction

General considerations (10); Basic principles (4)
The Bible itself gives us some examples
The purpose of interpretation
Why is sound interpretation important?

I. *Interpreting the Scripture Grammatically*

Sentence structure; word meanings
The literal sense and the intended sense
Intended sense in prophetic sections
Allegorical excesses
Interpretation is "one"; applications are "many"
Following the rules of language

II. *The Scripture Is Its Own Best Interpreter*

Is private interpretation permissible?

73

The *sola Scriptura* principle
How Scripture interprets Scripture
Word and thought parallels
How explain obscure passages?

Session Two

III. *Observe the Law of Context*

The importance of "staying in context"
Immediate and remote contexts
"Not good if detached" - - - -
"Never tear a passage out of context"
Learning from examples

IV. *Interpret the Scripture in Harmony with Itself*

Old Testament and New Testament are related like mold to
  medallion (examples)
The Law and Gospel motif of Scripture
Christ is the Key
Interpret in a complementary (not contradictory) way

V. *How to Understand Figurative Parts of Scripture*

Figures of speech in every living language
Examples from the Scriptures
Symbolism; Jesus' parables
Finding the "signals"

VI. *Read with Spiritual Discernment*

1 Cor. 2:9-14; the Holy Spirit still at work
Summary

Overview of Each Session

1. Opening worship: a hymn verse on the Word
2. Welcome and opening remarks:
   Reports and questions on preceding sessions and home
   study

3. Lesson outline on chalkboard;
   move directly into the lesson
4. Lead class through the sections chosen for the session
5. Let closing devotion grow out of lesson content: a prayer of
   thanks for insights gained

Further Suggestions for Teaching Each Session

Session One

Introduction

After recalling the 10 "preliminary considerations" of Chapter
8, indicate the four "basic principles" presented in Chapter 9. (Sections V and VI are not considered *basic* principles.) You may then
wish to awaken interest by alluding briefly to sample interpretations
within Scripture that show us the way. Spend more time on the four
purposes of interpreting Scripture. Then discuss with the class:
   a. The extremes in interpretation as presented by false liter-
      alism and radical liberalism.
   b. The phenomenon of denominationalism and the many di-
      visions in Christendom as related to different Bible inter-
      pretations.
      Examples:
      Roman Catholic: "The church is above the Bible."
         (Since Vatican II this is in the process of Modifi-
      cation.)
      Millennialists: "Literalness of prophecies."
      Reformed: "Law and Gospel sometimes confused."
      Lutheran: "Scripture must interpret Scripture." (More
         specifically, Law and Gospel are the interpretive
         keys. On Law and Gospel as derived keys for inter-
         preting Scriptures, see Bohlmann, *Principles of
         Biblical Interpretation in the Lutheran Confessions,*
         pp. 111–125, 138.)
      The different interpretations of Baptism and the Lord's
      Supper are another case in point.
   c. Every Christian is expected to be, and in a sense actually is,
      an interpreter. Luther claimed that every believer as a mem-

75

ber of the royal priesthood has the right and duty to explain Scripture (1 Peter 2:9-10). How is interpretation related to witnessing? family worship? nurture of children in the home?

I. *Interpreting Scripture Grammatically* (Ramm, pp. 133–135)

We have tried to simplify this chapter for laymen by selecting the four most essential points. Each writer in the field has his own way of organizing the principles. Thus Ramm in Chapter V lists six; Blair in Chapter II develops seven; Manley has eight (Ch. VI); Colson, in a fine chapter, describes six (Ch. IV).

In this section we bring together under the term "grammatical" several concepts: the meaning of words, their relation to each other in a sentence, the thrust of a sentence and paragraph. No one who ignores the grammatical sense deals honestly with Scripture.

The intended sense is what the interpreter is to seek. This is conveyed as the literal "then and there" meaning is discerned. Text, context, and usage will disclose if a given passage is to be taken literally (just what it says) or figuratively. The intended sense may be quite different than the literal meaning. Proper interpretation, however, must establish the literal sense first before the intended spiritual meaning (in a parable or prophecy) can be determined. Ramm summarizes this by saying that "nothing should be elicited from the text but what is yielded by the grammatical explication of the language." (*Protestant Biblical Interpretation*, p. 134)

In this section you may wish to have the class look at

a. Some connectives, for instance: 1 Cor. 15:58 (therefore) and 1 Cor. 16:1 (now)

b. What is the literal and then the intended sense of "leaven" in Matt. 16:5-12?

Ask the class to find the one intended sense of Gal. 6:7 or John 3:30, and then make several kinds of applications to the "here and now."

II. *The Scripture Is Its Own Best Interpreter* (Ramm, pp. 139–141)

Show from historical examples (for instance, Jehovah's Witnesses and Christian Science) how doctrines have been distorted by subjective, preconceived interpretations of Scripture. Then introduce 2 Peter 1:20-21 and the *sola Scriptura* principle. (See Formula of Concord, quoted in the study book, Ch. 7.)

Help the class see the value of using parallel passages intelligently and wisely. Select a number of verses with significant marginal references. Ask the class to report how further clarity is established by this practice, for instance, on justification by faith: Rom. 1:16-17; 3:28; 11:6; Eph. 2:8-9; Gal. 2:16. Show how a concordance helps us locate passages which deal with the same subject, for instance, the Good Shepherd (Psalm 23; John 10:11; etc.). In the *Reference Passage Bible* (New Testament, Moody Press reprint) the four gospels are shown in parallel columns with all major references to other Scripture printed out. The reference passages for all New Testament books are printed out alongside the text. With the suggested examples help the class distinguish word parallels from thought parallels.

Session Two

III. Observe the Law of Context

This is a major principle often disregarded. Examples from experience will suggest themselves. After working through the examples in the study text, impress the different epigrams for remembering this rule.

Ramm (pp. 135 – 138) distinguishes four circles of context. He quotes Barrows: "To interpret without regard to the context is to interpret at random; to interpret contrary to the context is to teach falsehood for truth." (*Companion to the Bible*, p. 531)

A good example of misquoting Scripture is the use of Col. 2:21 ("Do not handle, Do not taste, Do not touch") by the advocates of total abstinence. All that the context shows is that the use of legalistic regulations is contrary to the grace and freedom we have under the Gospel.

IV. Interpret the Scripture in Harmony with Itself

The Old and New Testaments are related structurally and doctrinally. This unity is the basis for the rule that Scripture should not be interpreted in contradiction to itself, as the school of historical criticism has done. This rule takes into account the "analogy of faith," that is, it calls for meaning in accordance with the basic teaching of the Christian faith. The "analogy of Scripture" principle calls for an interpretation that is in agreement with the general teaching of Scripture, for instance, its Law and Gospel message. Evangelical interpretation should proceed "in the light of Christ and the Gospel." The fulfillments recorded in Matthew illustrate this rule of interpretation. Get reports from the class.

James Smart, in *The Teaching Ministry of the Church* (p. 134), states this principle succinctly for the interpreter:

> He has to listen in faith to the words of the Old Testament for the voice that he can recognize as the voice of the same Lord whom he knows in Jesus Christ. He must read with discrimination, knowing that all parts are not of equal value to him. To read without discrimination, as though the Old Testament in every detail were equally authoritative for Christians, is to read as though one were not a Christian but a Jew, and, if followed to its logical conclusion, the approach would lead to some such aberration as an insistence that Christians observe the dietary and ritual laws of the Jewish religion.

Illustrate with examples some seeming contradictions.

As a summary of this section you may wish to put on the chalkboard the following illustration: Draw two pages side by side. Label the one Old Testament and the other New Testament. Then draw in outline the face of Christ so that it takes in parts of both pages. Write below: "Christ is the key to Scripture. He gives unity to the Old and New Testaments."

V. How to Understand Figurative Parts of Scripture (Ramm, pp. 141 – 142; 196 – 219)

Considerable time should be allowed for this section.

First get the class to define some of the terms used to distinguish various figures of speech. Presenting a few examples from a newspaper or magazine will make your point clear. Or pick up some examples from common speech.

The allegorists of the Alexandrian school beclouded the whole field of Biblical interpretation for about a thousand years. Luther broke sharply with this abuse of Scripture.

Typology is properly employed when we note and follow New Testament usage with regard to Old Testament figures. Examples are the brazen serpent (John 3:14-15) and sacrificial lambs prefiguring the Lamb of God (John 1:29). The whole Book of Hebrews abounds in types. Let the class discover some examples from Hebrews 9 and 10.

Typology has been "overplayed" by some interpreters. Many think it should be restricted to instances identified in the Bible as types. Others feel the New Testament shows the way and that the interpreter may exercise considerable liberty in finding parallels. One thing is clear: The typological prophecies of Christ are very significant and enrich the understanding of Scripture. Both Paul and Peter refer to many Old Testament types of Christ. We have already noted from Luke 24 and 1 Peter 1 the Christological nature of many Old Testament passages.

The exercise in the study book should help your students pick up the "signals" in the texts as they read the Bible.

Show by a few examples what it means to make a parable "walk on all fours." This is done when the interpreter introduces fanciful meanings for every small point of a parable, frequently obscuring the one main thrust which Jesus intended.

The parables emphasize two things, says Herbert T. Mayer, namely, "what God has done in Christ" and "the radical newness of life in His kingdom." (Ch. VI in *Interpreting the Holy Scriptures*)

Additional questions:

a. What are the points of comparison in the Kingdom parables?

Matt. 13:18-23_____ Matt. 13:33_____
      13:24-30_____   13:44_____
      13:31-32_____   13:47-49_____

b. How do Luke 15:1-2; 14:33; and 16:14 give us the key to the conversion parables in Luke 15?

Why did Jesus describe the Last Judgment (Matt. 25) in story form?

VI. Read with Spiritual Discernment

You may wish to begin with Jesus' promise to send the Holy Spirit to our side as Teacher, Revealer, and Interpreter (John 14:16; 15:26; 16:13). Through the written Word God still makes revelations to us today. Emphasize that Spirit-given faith makes understanding of the Scripture possible.

The class may wish to read the summary in unison.

References

Blair, E. P. *The Bible and You.* Nashville: Abingdon, 1953. Ch. 2.

** Bohlmann, Ralph A. *Principles of Biblical Interpretation in the Lutheran Confessions.* St. Louis: Concordia Publishing House, 1968.

** Colson, Howard P. *Preparing to Teach the Bible.* Nashville: Convention Press, 1959. Ch. 4.

Gaebelein, Frank E. *Exploring the Bible.* New York: Harper Bros., 1929. Ch. 10 (out of print).

* Heikkinen, Jacob W., and N. Leroy Norquist. *Helping Youth and Adults Know the Bible.* Philadelphia: Lutheran Church Press, 1962. Ch. 5.

* Manley, G. T. *The New Bible Handbook.* Chicago: Inter-Varsity Press. Ch. 6.

** Mayer, Herbert T. *Interpreting the Holy Scriptures.* St. Louis: Concordia Publishing House, 1967. 120 pp.

** Ramm, Bernard. *Protestant Biblical Interpretation.* Natick, Mass: Wilde, 1956. 274 pp.

Smart, James D. *The Teaching Ministry of the Church.* Philadelphia: Westminster Press, 1954. 207 pp.

Chapter 10

Overview of the Old Testament

TWO CLASS SESSIONS

Aim and Scope

The New Testament is more familiar to most Christians than is the Old. Some in your group may at best remember isolated incidents and stories about great characters who lived before Christ. Most may not understand the chronological sequence (the books of the prophets and apostles are *not* given in chronological order in your Bibles!). They may not sense what is most important and what is less significant to an understanding of God's acts in and through His people over more than four millennia. The Old Testament period covers a great span of human events. To understand them, we must consider both God's activity in Israel and His guiding hand in the surrounding nations.

There are many aids which introduce, summarize, and outline each of the 39 Old Testament books. Treating the books individually would be difficult within the scope of one lesson. It might divorce many books from their historical setting and thus fragmentize more than unify the Old Testament for the reader. Instead the approach of major concepts and larger general categories was chosen. It is more helpful in seeing the Old Testament as a whole.

The aim therefore is to help the student get an airplane view of the Old Testament — of the whole mountain range and not just of a few peaks. It is to help him see the hand of God in the diverse events and the roles of kings and prophets. The student is to find salvation history *(Heilsgeschichte)* rather than incidental stories. As a Christian he is to look at the Old Testament in the light of the New. This is the way of the New Testament itself.

Procedures for Two Class Sessions

1. Where students have become disciples (learners) who make it a rule to do reading before and after each class session, it should be possible to get at least two readings of the chapter: sections I to III before and after the first session, sections IV to VII before and after the second session. *This much reading should be required!* A course like this demands readers and students, not mere auditors. Those who fulfill this requisite will be thankful to you for what they have learned. Make each section relevant and exciting.

2. The thorough teacher will be tempted to expand at every point as his mind is stimulated. Obviously, to cover each paragraph with additional remarks is impossible timewise. Nor can all references be looked up and read in class. Since this is a textbook for home reading and constant reference, the leader must find his role as guide and resource person. How much knowledge can he take for granted?

3. Divide the chapter into two sections: (1) introduction and parts I – III, and (2) parts IV – VII. (Keep the functions of priests, kings, and prophets together.) The class may wish to use an extra (or third) session to discuss the "Thumbnail Sketches of Books of the Old Testament," pages 149 – 163 of the study book. This can be done by taking up the major divisions: Pentateuch, Historical Books, Wisdom and Worship Literature, Major Prophets, Minor Prophets.

4. Put the outline on the chalkboard, and call attention to several major ideas. Look up several key texts in each of the divisions, closing each with "meaning for the Christian." Include on chalkboard the most significant Bible references to be read in class. Be selective.

5. Do a time-line diagram of the Old Testament on the chalkboard. The class fills in the chief characters and events as the lesson progresses. The chart will be helpful, but you must be selective. Apply as you move along. See chart in study book.

6. Get good dialog with the class in each major area. Two or three good questions on each are needed. For instance, part I: How do chs. 1 – 11 of Genesis give you a better view of the world? of man? of the human predicament? Why is this a prologue to history?

7. There is no substitute for good preparation. The best book for this is deDietrich's *God's Unfolding Purpose* (see references); for session one, pages 27–83; for session two, pages 85–147. It sees the Old Testament in the light of the New Testament, yet allows the Old Testament to keep its own character and context.

Teaching Outline for Two Sessions

Session One

Introduction

I. *The Prologue:* The Beginning
   The Bible's prologue and epilogue
   Creation accounts, Old Testament – New Testament
   Man's place in the universe
   Sin and the human predicament
   The growth of sin; of civilization
   "Book of Beginnings"

II. *The Call of a People*
   God calls Abraham to faith
   The Sons of Jacob in Egypt
   The call of Moses to be deliverer of Israel
   The exodus and redemption by God
   Key to all Christian history

III. *The Covenant of God with His People*
   God's everlasting covenant
   Chesed – steadfast love, common faith
   Willing obedience – the people's part (Ten Commandments)
   The Law and the Gospel: How related?
   The promise of a new covenant, Jeremiah 31
   Israel and the covenant, Nehemiah 9

Session Two

IV. *The Priests – Worship in the Old Testament*
   Altars, offerings, priesthood (types)

Festivals (Leviticus 23) and a rhythm of worship
Tabernacle, temple, synagogue
Leviticus, Psalms
Teaching the faith to the family
Not religiosity but devoted hearts

V. *The Kings of Judah and Israel*

Joshua and entry into the Promised Land
The period of judges
The demand for a king—the monarchy
The divided kingdom: Judah and Israel
The everlasting kingdom (Christ)
Overview in the charts

VI. *The Prophets and Their Role*

Israel and Judah taken captive (exiles)
Who were the prophets?
Oral and writing prophets
What was their function? (threefold); searchlights
Return from Babylon—Ezra and Nehemiah
Between the Testaments
A greater Prophet—Christ—Deut. 18:15, 18

VII. *Christ the Climax*

God controls history
The Messiah promised
God kept His promises
Summaries: Joshua 24; Nehemiah 9; Acts 13:16-43

Overview of Each Session

1. Opening of session and worship: Ps. 119:18.
2. Introduction of lesson
3. The lesson
4. Assignment and preview
5. Closing devotion: Use one of the Passover psalms (113—118).

84

Further Suggestions for Teaching Each Session

Session One

Introduction

State the aim as given in the leaders manual, then refer in a few sentences to the "airplane approach" to the Old Testament and its value before proceeding to more detailed study.

I. The Prologue

Chapter 12 of the study guide contains a diagram which visualizes the prologue and epilogue of the Holy Scriptures. Invite the class to make the last three chapters an adventure into the drama of God's self-revelation. This is not the time to get lost in a debate on the details of creation. The class is to see "wholes." Look up some creation references in other books of Scripture. Focus on man's failure to meet God's test. The human predicament is the reason why God acted throughout history for man's salvation. Refer to all of Genesis as the "book of beginnings." What perspective of God, world, life, and man does this section give? Suppose we didn't have the first book of the Bible? You may wish to show the relation between Genesis 1 and 2 and John 1:1-5. Relate the creation account to the wisdom of God, the nobility of man as first created, the immensity of the universe, and the wonder of life. Recapture the wonder of it, as Luther does in his explanation of the First Article.

II. The Call of a People

God gives signs of His love and mercy already in Genesis 1 – 11, but a plan of gigantic proportions begins with the call of Abraham and the patriarchs and their families as God's chosen people. The plan continues to the end of time (1 Peter 2:9-10; Rev. 1:6). Don't get lost in a recital of the plagues in Egypt. Focus on the deliverance from bondage by the mighty hand of God. The exodus event (rehearsed again and again in Scripture) is a prototype of Christ's redemptive work, as is the Passover meal initiated in Egypt. Close with the fourfold meaning of "being God's people." How conscious are we daily of being God's New Testament Israel? Do we, as His purchased people, have a keen sense of mission? How is this related to the stewardship of life?

85

III. The Covenant of God with His People

There are some 275 entries of "covenant" in Young's *Analytical Concordance*. It is a concept that runs through both Testaments. Have we recognized its great significance? Have the class look up a few basic references. Introduce God as initiator who acts purely out of grace *(chesed)*. Help the group see that God gave the Ten Commandments to His people as guides for a life of willing obedience. By such a life they were to show their relation to God and man, to show that they were a "set-apart people of God." This is the place to teach that breaking the Law demands reconciliation (sacrifices), that keeping it demands God's Spirit in the heart. The New Testament era is a time when God's Spirit fully rules the heart (Jeremiah 31; Pentecost). Nehemiah 9 supplies a good summary. For a fuller treatment of the Biblical use of "covenant" consult a Bible word book (Richardson's *A Theological Word Book of the Bible).*

Session Two

IV. The Priests — Worship in the Old Testament

Your class will think of worship as we now have it in Christian churches. Our worship centers on Word and sacraments. It is characterized by teaching, preaching, the receiving of divine grace, the giving of praise, and the offering of self and money. How was Old Testament worship quite different? Leviticus 16 and 23 will be good preparation reading. Old Testament worship included emphases on God's holiness, man's uncleanness, and the need for atonement and reconciliation. It provided for a rhythm of daily, weekly, monthly, and annual worship functions. Focus on the prophetic, Christological aspects of these worship activities. Have the class read a few of the basic Scripture passages. Refer to the teaching functions carried on by parents in the home (Joshua 24:15; Deut. 6:4-9), and by priests (Lev. 10:8-11) as they went through all the cities teaching (2 Chron. 17:9; Neh. 8:1-2, 7-9). The synagogue school (after 500 B. C.) focused on reading and discussing the Law and the Prophets. Teaching and exhortation was done on occasion in solemn convocations, but evidently not in sacrificial services on the Sabbath. Briefly describe the functions of priests and Levites (see a Bible dictionary or read an "introduction to Leviticus"). If time permits, put the floor plan of the Old Testament temple on the chalkboard. You might use one of the psalms used in Jewish Passover observances for opening or closing of the session. (Psalms 113–118)

V. The Kings of Judah and Israel

The leadership of Joshua and the conquest of Canaan (never really completed) should be briefly sketched. The class may read Joshua 24:14-18. God gave His people leaders: first the "judges," who were led by the Spirit in a turbulent period, then the three kings of the monarchy. Capsule summaries of the reigns of Saul, David, and Solomon may be given (but do not get lost in biographical incidents). It is important to point out the dissension and division which caused the kingdom to be split. Note also the defections to idolatry, the alignment with Gentile nations, and the conflicts with them. There was much infiltration of pagan customs and religious concepts (Ahab and Jezebel, for instance). Use the charts to give an overview, and show the relationship between these kings and the King of kings, Jesus Christ, and His everlasting kingdom. (2 Sam. 7:13, 16; note the references to Jesus as Son of David, Matt. 22:42-45; as King, Matt. 27:11, 29, 37, 42; Rev. 17:14; 19:16) Study the charts, study book, pages 171–176.

VI. The Prophets and Their Role

Determine which paragraphs of this section are vital for understanding the mission of the prophets. Underscore salient sentences. The prophets, like John the Baptist, were "voices in the wilderness." They had no place in the temple services. They preached in the gate and in the marketplace. Like Ezekiel, they were "watchmen on the walls of Zion" (Ezekiel 33), calling God's people back to their covenant obligations. Select two or three classical paragraphs from a prophetical book (Amos, for instance) for dramatic reading in class. The prophets had a strong sense of social justice. They saw through the thin veneer of ceremonials, traditions, and perfunctory worship. Introduce both the nonwriting and writing prophets. Outline their functions as private counselors to kings and as public witnesses to Israel. This section includes paragraphs which briefly refer to the return from Babylon, the rebuilding of Jerusalem, the Apocrypha, the Maccabees, the intertestamental period, the rise of the scribes, Pharisees, Essenes. Use the charts as a review, and close with references to Christ, who is not only Priest (worship), King (ruler), but also Prophet (teacher). The charts do not list all the nonwriting prophets.

VII. Christ the Climax

The world and man are not accidents of blind fate. God is the Lord of history (also today). Israel's materialism lives on in our age (also in the church). But God is faithful. He wants to use us in His mission. Will we let Him? Close with selected verses from Acts 13:16-43.

Refer to "Thumbnail Sketches of Old Testament Books." (See Supplement)

References

See Charts of the Old Testament Era at end of the study book.

Archer, Gleason L. *A Survey of Old Testament Introduction.* Chicago: Moody Press, 1964, 507 pp. Various theories about the Old Testament are examined by a responsible Christian scholar; an introduction and outline of the 39 Old Testament books.

** deDietrich, Suzanne. *God's Unfolding Purpose.* Philadelphia: Westminster, 1960. Recommended for every teacher of this course. See Chs. I to VI. Note the following pages: 61, 62, 71, 81, 82, 83, 101 – 103.

* *Introduction to the Bible,* Vol. 1 of *The Layman's Bible Commentary.* Foreman, Kelly, Rhodes, Metzger, Miller. Richmond: John Knox Press, 1959. 171 pp.

** Manley, G. T. *The New Bible Handbook.* Chicago: The Inter-Varsity Fellowship, 1950. Pp. 77 – 114.

New Bible Dictionary, The, ed. J. D. Douglas. Grand Rapids: Eerdmans, 1962. 1,400 pp. One of the best of the modern dictionaries.

Richardson, Alan. *A Theological Word Book of the Bible.* London: SCM Press, 1957.

Schultz, Samuel J. *The Old Testament Speaks.* New York: Harper & Row, 1960. 437 pp. View of a careful, critical, but conservative scholar.

Tasker, R. V. G. *The Old Testament in the New Testament.* Philadelphia: Westminster, 1962. 174 pp.

Von Allmen, J. J. *A Companion to the Bible.* New York: Oxford University Press, 1958.

Chapter 11

How God Fulfilled His Covenant

TWO CLASS SESSIONS

Aim and Scope

Before examining the contents of the 27 New Testament books the student needs to have what surveyors call bench marks. A bench mark is a mark cut into some fixed object, such as a rock, to serve as a starting point or guide in determining altitudes or distances. This lesson is to supply the student with such starting points for understanding the New Testament.

The purpose of the chapter is to help the student see the relation between the Testaments and recognize the distinctive, unifying teachings in the Gospels, the Book of Acts, and the letters of the New Testament. In brief, it is to give the class an introduction to the New Testament.

Too frequently Bible readers get lost in little details, in incidental points of a narrative, or in the many events reported. They are like children who lose their way in a forest. Someone must help them find the main path. This is the challenging task of the leader. Help your class find the markers along the way. We might also speak of this as "finding our Lord's footprints in the New Testament."

Procedures for Two Class Sessions

1. How make discoverers of your class when you have two four-point sessions? How much of each section can you draw out of the class? How many of the points do you think the class already understands? Does the understanding rest on previous knowledge or experience? Must you provide the experience by letting group members find the facts in relevant texts? By first answering these questions you will better be able to choose procedures that fit your class.

2. Taking the introduction and sections I to IV into your first session will give you enough content for a challenging lesson. In the field test of this book the respondents were especially appreciative of the deeper insights gained about the relation between the Testaments. Section II is similar to a section in Chapter 7 but not identical. The class may wish to ask for additional information. "The kingdom of God" idea, so prominent in Jesus' conversations, is not easily identified. See a Bible word book for additional treatment. "The New Age of the Spirit" opens up other vistas of the Spirit's operation in the church today. Reading through the Book of Acts will impress again the prominence of the Holy Spirit in the life of the church.

3. The last four sections (V to VIII) focus more on the person and work of Christ and the new life in Christ.

4. Should the class feel that all eight sections cover already familiar ground and can be completed in a single session, you might use the second period to discuss the "Thumbnail Sketches of New Testament Books" under four divisions: Gospels, Acts, Letters, Revelation. Or this material may be reserved for a *third* session. At any rate, call attention to this supplement, pages 164–170 of the study book. Unfortunately many church members have never been given an introduction to the New Testament and cannot really distinguish one epistle from another. Another option is to close the entire course (after Ch. 12) with a closer look at the individual books of the New Testament.

Teaching Outline for Two Sessions
Session One

Introduction

1. Old Testament Markers: Prologue, Covenant, Israel, Exodus, Kings and Prophets, Exile, Restoration
2. New Testament Markers: What is distinctive of the New Testament? Were the covenant promises fulfilled?

I. *The Relation Between the Covenants*

Harmony of Scripture; importance of the Old Testament
Two Testaments (Covenants); Old and New Israel
Relation between Old and New Testaments (references)

II. *How and Why the New Testament Came into Being*

Jesus left no written record; apostles did
How Luke and the evangelists were led to write
How the letters came into being
Why was a written record necessary?

III. *With Christ the Kingdom Has Come*

"The time is fulfilled—the Kingdom has come"
What is meant by "kingdom of God"?
Message and demonstration of Christ the King
Entrance into and life in this kingdom
Everlasting kingdom—greater than David's or Solomon's

IV. *The New Age of the Spirit*

A new era—not a religion of laws
A theology of forgiving grace and a new heart
The fulfillment—the gift of the Holy Spirit
We still receive the same Spirit

Session Two

V. *The Person and Work of Christ*

The New Testament: Book of Jesus Christ
Jesus interpreter of the Law; proclaimer of the Gospel
Salvation by grace—illustrated
Call to faith in Christ (commitment)
The Sermon on the Mount: what is it?

VI. *Christ Crucified—the Heart of the Gospel*

The cross—foolishness and stumbling block
Morality, religion, Christianity
Not a mere "ethical religion"
Key doctrine: Christ died and rose for our salvation

VII. *The New Life in Christ*

Justification by faith—a dynamic faith
Faith at work in acts of love
Redeemed *from*, redeemed *for*

91

VIII. *The Pinnacle of Fulfillment*

Jesus the "Fulfiller" heralded by John the Baptist
Alienation ended — new life begins
Who is Jesus Christ?

Overview of Each Session

1. Friendly opening conversation and reports on reading and studying. Indicate how many sessions will be used to discuss Chapter 11
2. Introduction to the lesson ("markers") and opening prayer ("finding our Lord's footprints in the New Testament")
3. The lesson: How God fulfilled His promise ("An Introduction to the New Testament")
4. Reference to "Thumbnail Sketches of New Testament Books"
5. Summary, assignments, closing prayer

Further Suggestions for Teaching Each Session

Session One

Introduction

Why do surveyors use bench marks? What are some significant markers for understanding the broad outline of the Old Testament? Put class responses on chalkboard. Ask the class to name some distinctive markers of the New Testament.

I. The Relation Between the Covenants

The Bible (Old and New Testaments) has but one purpose and message. It speaks of one people. Christ cannot be understood apart from the Old Testament. Why? Help your class see this fundamental interrelatedness. The writings of the evangelists and apostles are filled with references to the Old Testament. See our Lord's references to the Old Testament as listed in Manley's *The New Bible Handbook* (pp. 4, 13 f., 71, 107, 152, 266, 276, 415, 442 – 455). Help the class find a few in Matthew and Luke. The "covenant" theme likewise runs through the two Testaments. Ask a stimulating question on each paragraph of this section, for instance: Could Christians understand Christ without the Old Testament? The two Testaments fit together like mold and medallion. Can we afford to neglect the Old Testament?

II. How and Why the New Testament Came into Being

The human side of the Bible is sometimes missed. God used ordinary persons and circumstances to give us the New Testament record. Have your class discover the apostolic message *(kerygma)* from Acts 10:34-43. How did it come to be written? (Luke 1:1-4). Give reasons why the New Testament writings were necessary to interpret God's mission to mankind.

The New Testament is the authentic source for Christian doctrine. It is the means for constant renewal and reformation. Every generation may get a fresh supply of the Gospel by a responsible use of the New Testament. Speculative theology must ever be under the judgment of responsible Biblical theology. Christians of the 20th century must know their New Testament, not only to evaluate all teaching but especially to understand life and their mission in this era.

Why are translations and distribution of the Bible so necessary for the achievement of the Christian mission in our times? Do we as a church recognize this in our mission strategy?

A few well selected questions will open up this section and enlist class response.

III. With Christ the Kingdom Has Come

For additional material on the New Testament use of "kingdom of God" (Matthew) or "kingdom of heaven" (Mark and Luke), consult a Bible word book (von Allmen or Alan Richardson) or a Bible dictionary. It is most important that the Old Testament background for our Lord's work be recognized. Consider, for instance, the many times Jesus is called Son of David. (See a concordance.) Many had then — and many have today — false understandings of God's kingdom (millennialism), of the true nature of Christ's kingdom (kingdom of grace, not of Law), and how man becomes a subject in it (John 3:3-5). The miracles of Jesus gave evidence of His kingship. (Of the 661 verses of Mark's Gospel, 105 make some reference to miracles!)

Why was Jesus' teaching of the kingdom of God considered "radical"? Is it so considered today? Why is this concept vital for understanding the New Testament?

IV. The New Age of the Spirit

Why did Jesus' teaching differ so sharply from the teachings of the scribes and Pharisees? Trace Jesus' penetrating analysis of the sinful human heart to His desire to show that the spirit of a person is determinative of his character (not the food that he eats, but the thoughts of his heart). Christ looks at the heart. How alone can man get this "new spirit"? How were the prophecies of Joel and Jeremiah fulfilled at Pentecost? how since then? The New Testament ushers in the age of "the new man in Christ" (2 Cor. 5:17; Eph. 2:8-10). Every page of the Book of Acts shows God's Spirit at work. How does God's Spirit work in our lives today?

Session Two

V. The Person and Work of Christ

Jesus did not discard the Ten Commandments. He used the Law and interpreted it. He taught that the spirit of the Law went beyond outward compliance and exposed inner attitudes of the heart. In doing so Jesus accentuated every man's guilt. He made bankrupt the doctrine that man can be saved by his own "righteousness." He paved the way for an understanding of the Gospel of grace and its acceptance by God-given repentance and faith. Let the class discover how much of the four gospels is devoted to the suffering, death, and resurrection of Christ. Someone might read through Acts, or one of the letters, and underscore every reference to the Atonement. This would show the centrality of this doctrine. Rev. 1:5 is a good summary. Help the class get a correct view of the Sermon on the Mount as an interpretation of life under the Gospel.

VI. Christ Crucified — the Heart of the Gospel

Discuss the statement by B. W. Anderson to drive home the distinctive nature of Christianity. Many so-called Christians still confuse morality and religion with Christianity. Assign beforehand the key words (redemption, reconciliation, etc.) to individuals for short definitions. Select four or five of the indicated texts for reading in class.

VII. *The New Life in Christ*

Help the class discover the centrality of justification by faith in the New Testament (Rom. 1:16-17; Gal. 2:16; Eph. 2:8-9). Show that a living faith is always active in a life of good works. This is part of its in-built nature and power. Faith is dynamic and life-changing. How do the Scripture references teach this? Have we experienced it for ourselves? Are we demonstrating to others that the kingdom of God has come to us?

VIII. *The Pinnacle of Fulfillment*

The words of Zechariah, the preaching of John the Baptizer, the express statements of Jesus, His teachings (parables) and works (miracles) all declare that the Messiah has come in the person of Jesus. God's promises, given through the ages, have been fulfilled in history with the incarnation of His Son. What new convictions have we gained from this chapter? What new commitment for our mission? What new insights into the nature of Christian faith and life?

We may speak of the Beatitudes in the Sermon on the Mount as "the ethics of grace." God gives the Kingdom to those who accept Him in humble faith. The sermon begins with eight paradoxes (Matt. 5:3-10), presents six antitheses (5:21-48), and gives directives for the Christian's life (chs. 6–7) and mission (5:13-16).

"Thumbnail Sketches of New Testament Books" (See Supplement)

This supplement in the study book, pages 164–170, is intended: (1) to supply more insights into the differences in content and nature of New Testament books, (2) to be an aid to the Bible student as he reads through his New Testament, and (3) to overcome the erroneous idea that "all the books are alike" and are to be approached in the same way. This should serve as an often-used section of this textbook and as part of a Christian's library.

Additional Notes

This chapter purposely emphasizes the theology of the New Testament and its central message. The proclamation of the apostles (*kerygma*) (Acts 10:34-43) included: (1) the age of fulfillment has come; (2) it happened through the life, death, and resurrection of Jesus; (3) Jesus by His resurrection and ascension was exalted as head of the new Israel; (4) the Holy Spirit in the church is a sign of the presence of the risen Lord; (5) the Messianic age will reach its consummation with the return of Christ; (6) therefore the listener is to repent and believe the Gospel.

The New Testament would have us see Jesus as the clue to the true nature of God and the true nature of man. He is the bridge across the gulf which man's failure to be what he was meant to be creates between himself and God.

As the founder of a new community, the church, Christ inaugurated a new order, the people of God, where men and women, bound in fellowship with Him and in loyalty to the way of life He indicated, may live in a new relationship to God and to each other by faith. Through Christ the way to God has been opened up, men's lives can be changed, and barriers of race and class can be broken down. The power of evil, pain, and death may be overcome as Christ Himself has overcome them. (O. K. Storaasli, *The Bible Book of Faith*, p. 109)

References

* Achtemeier, Paul J., and Elizabeth. *The Old Testament Roots of Our Faith.* Nashville: Abingdon, 1962.

Bell, Alvin E. *The Gist of the Bible Book by Book.* Grand Rapids: Zondervan, 1961.

Bright, John. *The Kingdom of God.* Nashville: Abingdon, 1953.

** deDietrich, Suzanne. *God's Unfolding Purpose.* Philadelphia: Westminster, 1960. Pp. 251 – 270.

Douglas, J. D., ed. *The New Bible Dictionary.* Grand Rapids: Eerdmans, 1962.

Franzmann, Martin H. *The Word of the Lord Grows.* St. Louis: Concordia, 1961.

* Huggenvik, Theo. *Your Key to the Bible.* Minneapolis: Augsburg, 1944.

** *Introduction to the Bible*. Vol. 1 of *The Layman's Bible Commentary*. Foreman, Kelly, Rhodes, Metzger, Miller. Richmond: John Knox Press, 1959.

** Manley, G. T., et al. *The New Bible Handbook*. Chicago: The Inter-Varsity Fellowship, 1950. Pp. 265–318.

Richardson, Alan. *A Theological Word Book of the Bible*. London: SCM Press, Ltd., 1957.

Von Allmen, J. J. *A Companion to the Bible*. New York: Oxford University Press, 1958.

(Film: *Our Bible: How It Came to Us*. New York: American Bible Society. Part I: "Formation of the Bible." 25 min.)

Chapter 12

Overview of the New Testament

TWO CLASS SESSIONS

Aim and Scope

You have helped your group see the relation between the Old and New Testaments and learn how and why the New Testament came into being. Your class has discovered some characteristic concepts of the New Testament, namely: kingdom of God, new age of the Spirit, God's grace in Christ, Gospel as good news, new life in Christ, and fulfillment of the covenant promises in Christ. You are now ready to move your students into the basic content of the New Testament's 27 books.

The aim of these sessions is to develop a general acquaintance with the New Testament, so that the student can distinguish between its four types of books; to give sufficient insight into these books to awaken reader interest, that is, to develop a better frame of reference and give a general introduction to the New Testament.

Personalizing This Lesson

Make the lesson "come alive" for the students. In the study book the last paragraph of each section relates to some personal application. The teacher helps by asking the right questions, for instance:

1. Why do the Gospels give so much space to Christ's Passion? What has this to do with our theology?
2. How are Matt. 28:16-20 and Acts 1:8 related to our personal witnessing? to the mission of our congregation?
3. When is our personal theology "Biblical" and "apostolic"?
4. What should "being the chosen of God" and "priesthood of all believers" mean for us personally?

5. What new impressions of the Old and New Testaments have you received from this course?

Preparation and Procedure

The leader prepares by giving the study text several careful readings, looking up all texts and writing in notes, references, key words, and other signals to recall content material or ideas he wishes to use. This frees him for teaching his own (internalized) lesson with his own background of illustrations and for giving attention to the concerns of the class.

Select, as the outline suggests, only a few key passages for use in class as you penetrate to the heart of each paragraph. Time limitations will demand omitting what can be examined more carefully at home.

The most helpful books are deDietrich's *God's Unfolding Purpose*, Manley's *New Bible Handbook*, and the books by Hunter (see references). Most instructors will appreciate these overview approaches that give syntheses of broader areas.

Draw from class members what they already know of the New Testament. Get reports on assignments, such as: the different beginnings and endings of the four gospels. The class session should consist of dialog between teacher and class, the former taking the initiative with apt questions. With the information and insight gained, fill out the outline on the chalkboard. This makes a live and rewarding lesson.

Teaching Outline for Two Sessions

Session One

Introduction

Old Testament, 1,000 years in making; New Testament, 50 years (A. D. 49–100). Christ is the "Bridge" between Old and New. He brought in a "new order." Through the New Testament runs one theme: "Christ died for our sins." In Old and New there is but *one* way to righteousness: by faith. (Romans 4:13, 22-25; 3:28)

I. The Four Gospels and Their Meaning

Their similarity and diversity (draw on descriptions of four gospels and your own background)

Matthew, Mark, Luke: By whom? To whom? Why? What?

Characteristics of John's Gospel

The content of the gospels—(Incarnation to Commission)

The Lord's Supper—the New Covenant

You and the gospels: Learn of Him, enlist, be trained!

II. The Early Church—Faith in Action (Book of Acts)

Witness of Jesus' followers (Acts 4:12; 10:34-43; 13:11-43; Old Testament references)

Pentecost—power of the Spirit (Jeremiah 31; Acts 1—2)

Ministries of Peter (Acts 1—12) and Paul (Acts 13—28)

Priesthood of all believers is in operation! (Acts 8:1-4; the key is 1:8)

As we are the church *on a mission,* we are "writing own book of acts"

III. The Letters—Theology Expressed

21 Epistles: three categories
To churches	13
To young co-workers	3
General letters	5

Situations which caused them to be written

Common message (1 Cor. 1:23-24; 15:3-4)

Each has a distinctive message (for key words see supplement)

Paul the great teacher (Eph. 1:3-14; Gal. 2:16; Eph. 3:14-19; 4:11-16)

"Salvation" used of (1) justification, (2) sanctification, (3) entry into heaven

Session Two

IV. God's People Today—the Church in the World

Community of God's people (Gal. 3:29; James 1:1; 1 Peter 2:9-10)

New Testament images and "pictures" of the church: body, etc.

Five functions given believers:
(1) witness (2) worship (3) grow in Christ
(4) minister [serve] (5) fellowship
Enabling power: the Spirit is given to believers

V. *The Triumph — to the Close of the Age*

Predictions of "last times" (Matthew 24 — 25)
Persecution and the Apocalypse (Book of Revelation)
(Seven churches; visions; not a timetable)
New heaven — Paradise regained — victory of church

VI. *The Hourglass of Salvation History* (Explain diagram)

Evaluation of the Course (Reports from Class Members)

Overview of Each Session

1. Opening
2. Welcome new members in group
3. Introduce the lesson (review of previous session)
   (Luther's experience)
4. Lead class through the lesson
5. Motivate and give clues for homework
6. Evaluation of course by class members (second session)

Further Suggestions for Teaching Each Session

Session One

I. *The Four Gospels and Their Meaning*

Choose your own way of beginning: When did you last read a gospel? What did you find? Why four gospels? How alike? How different? Show a "Harmony of the Gospels" (like the *Reference Passage Bible: New Testament* or W. F. Beck's *The Christ of the Gospels*). For each gospel let the class supply the basic information.

By whom? To whom? Why? What?

Your own notes might look like this:

Matt: Jewish world, Jesus, Son of Abraham and David, birth, fulfillments, "kingdom of heaven," parables, Sermon on Mount

Mark: for Romans, John Baptist, Ministering Christ (10:44-45), gospel of deeds and acts, concise, swift moving, training of the Twelve, "Son of Man"

Luke: introduction (1:1-4), to all mankind, birth, John Baptist, lost son, reference to women, a physician

John: Asia Minor and Greek world, miracles, "I am" discourses, conversations, theology in depth, great chapters and verses, Jesus called "the Word"

All Evangelists: Role of John the Baptist (Matt. 3:1-6) (Mark 1:1-4); genealogies of Matthew and Luke; ministry of our Lord in Galilee, Samaria, and Judea

General content: Incarnation; John Baptist; Baptism of Jesus; Jesus' ministries: healing and signs; teaching: parables and discourses; space given to His suffering, death, resurrection; the Great Commission and the Ascension

What is the place and significance of the Lord's Supper?

What do the gospels mean for us? (last paragraph of study, section I)

II. The Early Church — Faith in Action

Your outline will guide you. Relate opening of Acts to opening verses of Luke's Gospel. The keynote (Acts 1:8) should be visualized with concentric circles and related to our mission today. The message of the itinerant apostles was clear (4:12; 10:34-43). Assign this a week beforehand and ask for summary of it. Relate the Pentecost event to the new heart and new age promised in Jeremiah 31 and Joel 2.

Ask volunteers (week before) to give a 2-minute sketch of Peter's life (Cornelius, Acts 10), and a 3-minute sketch of Paul's life beginning with his conversion and citing his three missionary journeys. Fill in the gaps. Close with a reference to Acts 8:1-4 as demonstration of the priesthood (mission) of all believers. Give the quote from J. B. Phillips. Make an appeal to "be the church in the world of today."

III. The Letters — Theology Expressed

Help the class identify the three classes of letters. Then discover and discuss the situation which caused the writing of at least one letter. Show form of letters as written then. Discuss their purpose and use in the early church. From descriptions in the supplement (see study book) draw examples and key words of some of the chief letters. Draw on your own experience with them. What is the message they have for the church today? Give examples of Paul as teacher and his Christian growth goals (for instance, Col. 1:9-12). From a theological word book (Von Allmen's or Alan Richardson's) demonstrate the various uses of "salvation" in the New Testament.

Session Two

IV. God's People Today — the Church in the World

Confine your time to the connection between the Old and the New Testament people of God (passages); to letting the class suggest from memory various images or pictures of the church (vine and branches, body of Christ, etc.); and to the five functions of the people of God today, namely, witness, worship, growth in Christ, service, and fellowship. Point out that every Christian has all five functions.

V. The Triumph — to the Close of the Age

Look up "Apocalypse" or "apocalyptic" in a Bible dictionary or word book and read a short summary of the Book of Revelation for more detail. See supplement to this lesson. How does it apply to Christians today?

VI. The Hourglass of Salvation History

The diagram of the whole Bible illustrates its unity and gives an overview of Chapters 10 — 12.

Evaluation of Course

These sessions will bring to a close your class on LEARNING TO USE YOUR BIBLE. This suggests a class evaluation of what was learned and what skills were acquired. This can be achieved with four or five questions given to the class a week before the last session.

The evaluation sheet may use these questions:

1. How did book and class enlarge your understanding of the Bible?

2. What did they contribute to your personal faith and relation to God?
3. What new skills for reading and studying the Bible did you acquire?
4. Did the course make any difference in your personal or family use of the Bible?
5. Have you talked about the course to others and shared your learnings?

If a longer class period is available for the evaluation, your questions may touch on these points: new concepts, wider understanding, expanded knowledge, greater confidence for Bible reading and study, better identity of self with God's covenant people. As regards improved skills, try these points: attitude change toward the Bible's place in your life, new interest in group Bible study, more rewarding Bible *reading* and Bible *study* procedures. How will you use your new skills?

References

Aaseng, Rolf E. *The Sacred Sixty-Six*. Minneapolis: Augsburg, 1967.

Beck, Wm. F. *The Christ of the Gospels*. St. Louis: Concordia Publishing House, 1959.

Bell, Alvin E. *The Gist of the Bible*. Grand Rapids: Zondervan, 1961.

** Brown, Raymond B., and Velma Darbo. *A Study of the New Testament*. Nashville, Tenn.: Broadman Press, 1965. 192 pp.

** deDietrich, Suzanne. *God's Unfolding Purpose*. Philadelphia: Westminster, 1960. Pp. 151 to 270. This was found to be most helpful.

** Huggenvik, Theo. *Your Key to the Bible*. Minneapolis: Augsburg, 1944.

** Hunter, A. M. *Introducing the New Testament*. Philadelphia: Westminster Press, 1957.

_____. *Introducing New Testament Theology*. Philadelphia: Westminster Press, 1958.

Manley, G. T. *The New Bible Handbook*. Chicago: Inter-Varsity Fellowship, 1949.

Mayer, Herbert T. *The Books of the New Testament*. St. Louis: Concordia, 1949. Paper, 133 pp.

Reference Passage Bible: New Testament, The. (Four Gospels in parallel columns.) Chicago: Moody Press, 1967 (reprint).

Richardson, Alan. *A Theological Word Book of the Bible*. Chicago: Macmillan, 1957.

Tenney, Merrill C. *New Testament Survey*. Grand Rapids: Eerdmans, 1961.

Von Allmen, J. J. *A Companion to the Bible*. New York: Oxford University Press, 1958.